The ADHD Toolkit

Education at SAGE

SAGE is a leading international publisher of journals, books, and electronic media for academic, educational, and professional markets.

Our education publishing includes:

- accessible and comprehensive texts for aspiring education professionals and practitioners looking to further their careers through continuing professional development

- inspirational advice and guidance for the classroom

- authoritative state of the art reference from the leading authors in the field

Find out more at: **www.sagepub.co.uk/education**

The ADHD Toolkit

Linda Wheeler

Los Angeles | London | New Delhi
Singapore | Washington DC

SAGE Publications Ltd
1 Oliver's Yard
55 City Road
London EC1Y 1SP

SAGE Publications Inc.
2455 Teller Road
Thousand Oaks, California 91320

SAGE Publications India Pvt Ltd
B 1/I 1 Mohan Cooperative Industrial Area
Mathura Road
New Delhi 110 044

SAGE Publications Asia-Pacific Pte Ltd
33 Pekin Street #02-01
Far East Square
Singapore 048763

Library of Congress Control Number 2009933779

British Library Cataloguing in Publication data

A catalogue record for this book is available from the British Library

ISBN 978-1-84860-183-3
ISBN 978-1-84860-184-0 (pbk)

Typeset by C&M Digitals (P) Ltd, Chennai, India
Printed in Great Britain by CPI Antony Rowe, Chippenham, Wiltshire
Printed on paper from sustainable resources

Contents

Key to icons

Chapter objectives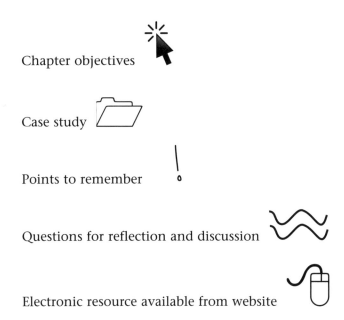

Case study

Points to remember

Questions for reflection and discussion

Electronic resource available from website

List of electronic resource materials

Wherever you see the [icon] icon, downloadable material can be found at www.sagepub.co.uk/wheeler for use in your setting. A full list of materials follows.

Acknowledgements

The schools involved in the case studies remain anonymous, but a special thank you must go to the head teachers, staff and students who provided a warm welcome and offered every assistance with the research.

I should like to acknowledge the assistance given by Wendy Quill and her colleagues in the undertaking of the school ADHD survey and the organisation of two ADHD study days.

In supervising the research, the overwhelming support and encouragement received over six years from Peter Wakefield and Professor Peter Pumfrey have been invaluable.

Many thanks to Jude Bowen and Amy Jarrold at Sage for all their help and encouragement.

Finally, neither the completion of the research nor the writing of this book would have been possible without my husband, David, who has had faith in me over the years and supported me every step of the way.

About the author

Linda Wheeler

Linda Wheeler is an ex-teacher in mainstream primary and special schools who has developed an interest in exploring and understanding more about the nature of ADHD from an educational perspective. She has recently completed a PhD at the University of Worcester in association with Coventry University, UK. So far two articles based on her research findings have been published in the journal *Emotional and Behavioural Difficulties*. Linda is a part-time lecturer in the Institute of Education, University of Worcester, Worcester, UK. She can be contacted at linda wheeler50@hotmail.com for further details of her research or advice on INSET training in schools.

How to use this book

This book is primarily based on the research undertaken for the author's PhD thesis and offers discussion of the theoretical issues surrounding the concept of ADHD as well as practical applications of the findings. The research was in two parts which ran concurrently. One part was based on detailed analyses of data from a question-naire survey on ADHD in all schools in a local authority, together with analyses of responses from delegates attending two ADHD study days at a university. The other part adopted a case study approach to gather in-depth data on situational and tem-poral variability in ADHD behaviour in school settings, enabling the identification of approaches and strategies for minimising such behaviour.

Where appropriate, extracts from the PhD research data are used to illustrate particular features. Anonymity has been ensured by the use of pseudonyms throughout the research and the book. From the inclusion of the details and views of real students and real-life situations in schools in addition to theoretical considerations, readers will be able to relate some of their own experiences to the research findings and strategies presented here in order to gain a clearer understanding of the issues raised. The book may be read as a whole, but would also suit individual readers or school groups wishing to focus on particular chapters or sections. A glossary provides a list of ADHD-related terms, acronyms and abbreviations used in the book. PowerPoint presentations (Appendix A, B and C) offer a brief explanation of the contents of each section of the book and may be used to facilitate staff training, for example on school INSET days. A further PowerPoint presentation (Appendix D) is included for use with parents. All four presentations are available as downloadable materials.

Throughout the book, and in Section 2 in particular, to avoid confusion, 'he' is used to describe a student with ADHD and 'she' for a teacher. This is obviously not always the case, but it reflects the higher number of boys with a diagnosis and the higher proportion of female teachers, particularly in early years and primary settings.

Foreword

At the time of writing it is approximately 16 years since the current version of the ADHD diagnosis was published. This version is of course only the most recent of a series of criteria published by the American Psychiatric Association dating back to the middle of the 20th century. It is also important to note that the American Psychiatric Association diagnosis of ADHD has many close similarities (and is identical in some respects) with the World Health Organization diagnosis of Hyperkinetic Syndromes which has a similar lengthy history. There are also claims that something very similar to these modern diagnoses can be traced back much further to the work of the appropriately named English physician George Still in the early 1900s (Barkley, 1997), and the Scottish physician Alexander Crichton, who was working at the overlap between the 18th and 19th centuries (Palmer and Finger, 2001). Furthermore, the nature of ADHD and related conditions, and interventions for them have been the subject of more scientific research than any other biopsychosocial disorder which is highly prevalent among children and young people (Barkley, 2005).

Given these uncontroversial facts, it is surprising that ADHD has been the subject of a sometimes heated debate, stimulated by individuals who question its legitimacy. A recent example of such a negative, anti-ADHD view is provided by Skidmore (2004), who writes:

> Given its long historical roots, and the undoubted existence of such psychological and medical conditions [as Down's syndrome and autism], it is likely that research into learning difficulties in the psycho-medical paradigm will continue to be conducted, that it will continue to exert an influence on the wider field, and that some of its findings will be found to be of use in the education of pupils who are affected by conditions which are generally recognised to have an organic basis. The difficulty arises when illicit attempts are made to apply this framework to an infinitely extensible set of putative syndromes or disorders for which reliable evidence of a neurological or organic base is lacking, and where 'diagnosis' rests on value laden, culturally-specific judgements about behavioural or cognitive norms. In the case of ADD [sic] it is arguable that the scientistic discourse of positivism and the rhetorical stance of authoritative objectivity which it engenders have been deployed to disseminate a biological determinist hypothesis for which empirical evidence is wanting, and to legitimise the practice of drugging defiant children into docility, using stimulants whose long-term side effects are unknown, in the service of a tacit project of social control.

> (Skidmore,2004, pp.3–4).

Skidmore's distaste for ADHD is not unique, Slee (1995) wrote something similar almost ten years earlier, and twenty years before him Schrag and Divoky (1975) wrote a book entitled: *The Myth of the Hyperactive Child, and Other Means of Child Control.* For the reader who has engaged with the educational and psycho-medical literature on ADHD these negative views are baffling. To portray ADHD as a biological determinist construct which not only lacks scientific credibility, but acts as a tool for inflicting harm on children and young people, is, to put it politely, at odds with what the research and theoretical literature relating to ADHD actually says. Writers who promote these views have either not understood the literature which seeks to illuminate ADHD, or they have failed to engage with it in the first place. If they did they would realise that the most negative life outcomes associated with ADHD (such as educational failure, relationship difficulties, delinquency and mental health problems) are associated with a failure to identify and intervene with ADHD early in a person's life. Further, they would realise that far from being a 'biological determinist hypothesis' ADHD is best understood as a biopsychosocial condition (Barkley, 2005); that is, a phenomenon that is the product of the dynamic interaction between inherited (genetic) characteristics and the social environment.

Fortunately, Linda Wheeler, whose book you are reading, has not only engaged with the literature on ADHD and understood it, she has contributed to it, both as an academic researcher and as a pedagogue. *The ADHD Toolkit* offers an extremely well researched guide to understanding and supporting students with ADHD in schools. One thing that any reader will be able to take from this text is that ADHD, far from being a bogus construct, is very real, both at the conceptual level and in terms of the day to day experience of the people who bear the diagnosis and those with whom they interact. This book will help the reader to understand the difference between the child who is disaffected, defiant and oppositional, and the child whose core difficulties reside in chronic problems of self regulation and concentration (ie. ADHD). It will also help the reader to understand how to translate these insights into practical strategies that will promote the positive social and educational engagement of students with ADHD. This is not to say that students with ADHD are not sometimes capable of being disaffected, defiant and oppositional. They can develop these characteristics when the core features of ADHD are ignored. Linda Wheeler's book will help the reader to realise that to adopt the view that ADHD is merely an excuse for mistreating 'defiant children' is not only ignorant, it is positively dangerous. Such an approach will *promote* defiance and disaffection, because it ignores the central cause of the initial difficulties.

I hope you will enjoy reading Linda Wheeler's book as much as I have. More importantly, I hope you will take from it its central message of compassion for students who experience ADHD and their need for understanding and informed intervention.

References

Barkley, R (1997) *ADHD and the Nature of Self Control*. New York: Guilford.

Barkley, R (2005) *ADHD: A Handbook for Diagnosis and Treatment*, 3rd Edition. New York: Guilford.

Palmer, E. and Finger, S. (2001) 'An early description of AD/HD: Dr. Alexander Crichton and "mental restlessness"', *Child Psychology and Psychiatry Review*, 6 (2): 66–73.

Schrag, P and Divoky, D (1975) *The Myth of the Hyperactive Child, and Other Means of Child Control*. London: Pantheon.

Skidmore, D (2004) *Inclusion*. Milton Keynes: Open University Press.

Slee, R. (1995) *Changing Theories and Practices of Discipline*. London: Falmer.

Introduction

In focusing on the following questions this introduction also identifies some of the issues discussed in the main sections of the book:

- **What** is ADHD?
- **Why** is there a need for this type of book?
- **Who** is the book aimed at?
- **How** is the book organised?
- **Why** *The ADHD Toolkit*?

What is ADHD?

Attention deficit hyperactivity disorder (ADHD) is a medical diagnosis that is applied to children, young people and adults who are experiencing significant behavioural and cognitive difficulties in important aspects of their lives. These difficulties can be attributed to problems of inattention, hyperactivity and impulsivity. Inattention is observed in behaviours such as seeming not to listen, not following through on instructions, being forgetful in daily activities, being easily distracted by extraneous stimuli and failing to complete tasks. Hyperactivity refers to excessive or developmentally inappropriate levels of activity, whether motor or vocal. Impulsiveness means that the individual acts or speaks without thinking and has difficulty waiting in turn to participate in games or answer questions in class. It can be argued that most children display these symptoms at some time, but in order to be considered for assessment and diagnosis of ADHD, the individual must display six or more symptoms of inattention and/or six or more symptoms of hyperactivity–impulsivity. Some of the three main symptoms must have been present before the child was 7 years old and symptoms should have been present for at least six months. They should occur in more than one setting (e.g. home and school). There should be clear evidence of significant impairment in social and academic functioning and they should not be accounted for by any other mental disorder (APA, 2000).

The theoretical basis of the nature of ADHD and its causes, prevalence and the effects of interventions are controversial areas of research and practice. The field has attracted considerable attention from professionals in the areas of education, psychology and health: 'During the last decade … ADHD has been one of the most widely observed, described, studied, debated and treated childhood disorders' (Kendall, 2000: 65). Internet searches have found evidence of a growing number of references to ADHD worldwide, although there are obvious limitations as to the validity of some of these sources. The most fundamental debate has centred on the reality or existence of ADHD. There are differing views as to the core symptoms and definitions of the features of the disorder. Various theories point to impairment in behavioural inhibition on executive functions, delay aversion, attentional bias and the lack of inhibitory control as underlying problems.

The use of medication continues to be one of the most controversial issues surrounding the concept of ADHD. There is a need for a multi-professional approach in the identification, assessment and management of ADHD. Professional opinion is often polarised, leading to disagreements between psychologists and education-alists, for example, as to the best course of treatment. There can be significant fluctuation in the severity of ADHD symptoms across settings and variability of behaviour over time. Situational and temporal variation in school may be influenced by task complexity, novelty and task stimulation, fatigue, the time of day and/or the degree of individualised attention being provided (Barkley, 2006).

Why is there a need for this type of book?

One of the major areas where ADHD behaviours can present problems is in the school setting: 'More than any other domain of major life activities, the educational sphere is devastatingly affected by this relatively common disorder' (DuPaul and Stoner, 2003, Foreword by Barkley: ix). In the current context of inclusive education, teachers in mainstream schools will be increasingly likely to experience involvement with students with special educational needs (SEN), including those deemed to manifest symptoms of ADHD. Schools are under pressure to raise academic standards while at the same time taking forward the inclusion agenda. Innovations including a National Curriculum, examination league tables, parental choice and school inspections can be problematic in the provision of inclusive education for students with ADHD.

In government guidance on inclusion there has been acknowledgement of the need for closer multi-agency cooperation, curriculum flexibility and teacher training in SEN (DfES, 2003, 2004; DCSF, 2007). There have been calls for increased investment in teacher education on ADHD at both the initial training stage and as part of in-service training so that all educational practitioners may be more able to meet the needs of individuals with ADHD (Cooper and Bilton, 2002). There is as yet little evidence of increases in relevant training for teachers and teaching assistants (Stewart, 2006).

Although numerous books and journal articles have been published on various aspects of ADHD, it is important that up-to-date research findings are disseminated and that more information and proactive strategies are made available to the teachers of today and tomorrow. This book begins with a short introduction to the concept of ADHD before focusing on offering practical guidance on observing and managing ADHD behaviour in mainstream schools. References to other literature and a list of useful organisations and websites aim to encourage further reading and research.

Who is the book aimed at?

The strategies and approaches described in this book could benefit all learners aged 3–18 years in educational settings from early years through to primary and secondary schools, both with and without a formal diagnosis of ADHD. The book will primarily be directed towards teachers, teaching assistants and support staff involved in mainstream education. It could be useful in Continuing Professional Development and INSET training, and also in teacher training institutions and on foundation, undergraduate and postgraduate courses and modules in education. The contents of the book will be of interest to other professionals involved in the management of individuals who display ADHD-type characteristics, including educational psychologists, health practitioners and social workers. The parents of students and some older students themselves will also find the book helpful, particularly with regard to the importance of effective home–school relationships.

How is the book organised?

Based primarily on a comprehensive review of relevant literature, Section 1 provides the reader with a basic understanding of the nature of ADHD. Chapter 1 begins by focusing on the general concept of the disorder, including the historical background, theoretical conceptualisations and current concerns. Chapter 2 offers a brief discussion on the use of medication. The need for a multi-professional approach in the identification, assessment and management of ADHD is considered in Chapter 3. Section 2, the most significant section, focuses on the school setting and draws on findings from up-to-date practice-based empirical research. The need for observation in school contexts together with full details and practical applications of two new systematic classroom observation schedules incorporating the *Diagnostic and Statistical Manual of Mental Disorders* (4th edition) (DSM-IV) diagnostic criteria for ADHD (APA, 2000) are included in Chapter 4. By examining observed variability in ADHD behaviour across settings and over time, Chapter 5 focuses on effective teaching approaches for students with ADHD. General classroom and behaviour management strategies which can be used in reducing specific ADHD symptoms and characteristics are highlighted in Chapter 6. Chapter 7 provides information on associated and coexisting difficulties. Section 3 examines the wider context, beginning with Chapter 8 which focuses on the importance of parental involvement and effective home–school relationships. Finally, Chapter 9 concludes by discussing the implications of the research findings and offering recommendations for future policy and practice.

Finally, why *The ADHD Toolkit?*

> **Dictionary definitions of 'toolkit':**
>
> 1. *Set of tools,* especially for a specific type of work, kept in a special box or bag.
> 2. *Information and advice:* a collection of information, resources and advice for a specific subject area or activity.

In one book *The ADHD Toolkit* includes everything necessary to increase awareness of the disorder and to equip busy educational professionals with sufficient theoretical knowledge of the concept of ADHD with which to make decisions regarding pedagogical and curricular flexibility. In addition the importance of developing effective multi-professional involvements is highlighted. An added advantage for those readers wishing to undertake further research is the inclusion of references, suggestions for further reading and a list of useful organisations and websites.

Section 1

Background to ADHD

1

The concept of ADHD

This opening chapter in Section 1 provides basic background knowledge of the concept of ADHD by highlighting several important and often controversial areas, beginning with differences in approaches to diagnosis of the disorder. Changes in terminology over time point to varying attitudes regarding the nature of ADHD. There is an examination of the multi-factorial causes as well as the variation in prevalence figures for the disorder. Coexisting social, emotional and educational difficulties often experienced by children with ADHD and the long-term prognosis are discussed. The chapter concludes by looking at medical, educational and social interventions used with individuals with ADHD, as well as listing some alternative and complementary interventions.

The 'Myth or Fact?' sheets (see Figures 1.1 and 1.2, also available as downloadable materials) offer a good starting point for the reader wishing to know more about the background of ADHD. Some of the following subsections are examined in greater detail in subsequent chapters.

Diagnosis

ADHD is a medical disorder and diagnosis is made by a qualified medical clinician (paediatrician or child psychiatrist) using one of two sets of diagnostic criteria currently in use. Traditionally in Europe and the UK the *International Classification of Diseases* (ICD-10), which refers to 'hyperkinetic disorder' (HKD) rather than ADHD, had been the preferred classification system (WHO, 1990). In recent years there has been more use of the fourth edition of the *Diagnostic and Statistical Manual of Mental Disorders* (DSM-IV) which is widely followed in the USA, Australia and other countries (APA, 2000). In the DSM-IV system the behavioural characteristics associated with ADHD do not represent three primary symptoms but two, with hyperactivity forming a single symptom group with impulsivity. This system is capable of identifying three main subtypes of ADHD (the first subtype is thought to be more common in girls than boys and the other two subtypes are more common in boys than girls):

ADHD: Myth or Fact?

1. ADHD is a medical disorder.

2. ADHD is an invention of modern western culture.

3. ADHD is genetic.

4. ADHD is simply caused by poor or inadequate parenting.

5. At least one child in a mainstream classroom will have ADHD.

6. More boys than girls are diagnosed with ADHD.

7. A child cannot have ADHD as well as another condition or disorder.

8. ADHD is a childhood disorder which disappears by puberty.

9. Unless you receive a diagnosis as a child, you cannot have ADHD as an adult.

10. The use of medication can be effective in treating ADHD.

Figure 1.1 ADHD: Myth or Fact? (Sheet 1)

ADHD: Myth or Fact?

1. **Fact.** Diagnosis is made by a qualified medical clinician whose assessment includes detailed information from parents and other professionals including teachers.

2. **Myth.** ADHD may have existed in some form or another since at least as far back as the nineteenth century.

3. **Fact.** In approximately 70 per cent of cases the disorder is inherited from a parent or other relative.

4. **Myth.** This lacks supportive evidence. It is believed that ADHD is caused primarily by neurological dysfunction.

5. **Fact.** Between 1 and 5 percent of school-aged children may have ADHD.

6. **Fact.** Estimates for the boy:girl gender ratio vary between 9:1 and 4:1.

7. **Myth.** Approximately 60 to 70 per cent of children with ADHD have comorbid or coexisting conditions of various types.

8. **Myth.** Around 70 to 80 per cent of children continue to exhibit significant deficits in attention and impulsivity compared to their adolescent peers. Between 30 and 70 per cent of people carry some or all of the ADHD traits into adulthood.

9. **Myth.** Although there cannot be an adult onset of ADHD, quite commonly the diagnosis is not made until adulthood. Adults with ADHD often have a history of under-achievement, low self-esteem and relationship problems.

10. **Fact.** When used as part of a multi-modal, multi-professional approach, medication is highly effective in reducing the core symptoms of ADHD in 80–95 per cent of cases.

 Figure 1.2   ADHD: Myth or Fact? (Sheet 2)

- the predominantly inattentive type (often known as ADD);

- the predominantly hyperactive–impulsive type;

- the combined type.

The main difference between diagnoses made using ICD-10 criteria and DSM-IV criteria is that ICD-10 focuses on extreme levels of hyperactivity and does not have a non-hyperactive subtype. The differences between the two sets of criteria mean that ICD-10 have been repeatedly shown to select a smaller group of children with more severe symptoms than those selected using DSM-IV. Munden and Arcelus (1999) are among those who advocate the use of DSM-IV criteria: firstly, to identify more children who may have significant impairment but do not satisfy ICD-10 criteria, but who could benefit from treatment and intervention. Secondly, the majority of international research is being carried out on patients who fulfil DSM-IV criteria and if UK clinicians wish to utilise evidence from such research they will have to apply it to the same clinical population.

A rigorous assessment is based on the child's past medical history, educational history, family history, physical examination and information from other professionals, including teachers and educational psychologists. Approaches used include observation of the child, both in the clinic setting and the school environment; in-depth interviews with the child, parents and teachers; aptitude testing and physiological and neurological testing; and the completion of behavioural rating scales. Symptoms emerge more clearly between the ages of 6 and 9 years. Findings from the school survey undertaken as part of the research show that the highest percentage of individuals was diagnosed in the 5–9 year age group. The four target students included in the six case studies who had received formal diagnoses of ADHD by the end of the research period were diagnosed as follows:

- David was diagnosed at the age of 4 years 4 months.

- Edward was diagnosed at the age of approximately 5 years.

- Carl was diagnosed at the age of 6 years 9 months.

- Adam was diagnosed at the age of 8 years 8 months.

History

ADHD may have existed in some form or another since at least as far back as the nineteenth century. One of the first professional reports of the disorder was probably in 1902 in *The Lancet* by George Still, a British paediatrician.

In the 1930s, behavioural disturbances were related to brain injury and in 1937 stimulant medication (amphetamine) was first used to treat a group of behaviourally disordered children. It was in the 1950s and 1960s that the term 'minimal brain dysfunction' was used, with the disorder no longer ascribed to brain damage but focusing more on brain mechanisms. Methylphenidate (Ritalin), introduced in 1957, began to be more widely used, particularly in the USA. During the 1960s the 'hyperactive child syndrome' became a popular label. Research in the 1970s suggested that attention and not hyperactivity was the key feature in this disorder and led to the establishment of 'attention deficit disorder' (ADD) as a category in the third edition of the

Diagnostic and Statistical Manual of Mental Disorders (DSM-III) published by the American Psychiatric Association (APA) in 1980. There have since been several reformulations of DSM, with the category of attention deficit hyperactivity disorder (ADHD) first used in 1987 and redefined in 1994, with a further text revision in 2000 (DSM-IV TR) (APA, 2000). The various name changes that the disorder has undergone over the years reflect changing conceptualisations of the nature of the condition.

In Sweden and other Scandinavian countries the term 'DAMP' (deficits in attention, motor control and perception) has frequently been used as a diagnosis. DAMP is a combination of ADHD and DCD (developmental coordination disorder, present in 50 per cent of ADHD cases). Sometimes the combined expression ADHD/DAMP is used (Gillberg, 2002).

Causes

Although there is no one single 'cause' of ADHD, it is believed that the disorder is caused primarily by neurological dysfunction. Research studies have found particularly low levels of activity in the neurotransmitters in the frontal lobes of the brain which control impulses and regulate the direction of attention. This means that children with ADHD often experience problems in inhibiting or delaying a behavioural response. The causes of this particular brain dysfunction in most cases appear to be genetic, with approximately 70 per cent of cases being inherited. Most children diagnosed with ADHD have a close relative (usually male) affected to some degree by the same problem. In studies of identical twins, both have ADHD in almost 90 per cent of cases, and siblings carry a 30–40 per cent risk of inheriting the disorder. Environmental factors such as brain disease, brain injury or toxin exposure may be the cause of 20–30 per cent of cases (Cooper and Bilton, 2002). Other suggested risk factors for ADHD include pregnancy and delivery complications, prematurity leading to low birth weight and foetal exposure to alcohol and cigarettes.

When seeking to explain the multi-factorial causes of ADHD, reference is often made to the interrelationship between *nature* and *nurture*. The concept is described by many as a bio-psycho-social disorder. This means it may be viewed as 'a problem which has a biological element, but that interacts with psychosocial factors in the individual's social, cultural and physical environment' (Cooper, 2006: 255). Biological factors include genetic influences and brain functions, psychological factors include cognitive and emotional processes and social factors include parental child-rearing practices and classroom management (BPS, 2000).

Prevalence

Although figures vary according to where and when studies are carried out and the diagnostic criteria used, it appears that ADHD is present throughout the world. It occurs across social and cultural boundaries and in all ethnic groups. International estimates of prevalence rates vary, and include suggestions of between 3 and 6 per cent of children and young people (Cooper, 2006). American data collected in 2003 suggests prevalence rates of between 5 and 8 per cent in children aged 4 to 17 years old (Goldstein, 2006). One interesting theory put forward for national differences in countries such as North America and Australia is that 'in past centuries, the more impulsive risk takers were more likely to emigrate or become involved in antisocial activity that would have led to their transportation. This group would probably have had a higher incidence of ADHD, which would have been inherited by subsequent generations' (Kewley, 2005: 13).

In the UK it is difficult to ascertain accurate national prevalence figures. The breakdown of SEN figures provided in government statistics does not include a discrete category for ADHD. Taylor and Hemsley (1995) suggest that 0.5–1 per cent of children in the UK have ADHD or hyperkinetic disorder (HKD). It was recently reported that there were 4,539 children and young people diagnosed with ADHD known to NHS services in Scotland. This is approximately 0.6 per cent of the school-aged population (NHS Quality Improvement Scotland, 2008). Government guidance for schools in Northern Ireland refers to ADHD occurring in 1–3 per cent of the population (Department of Education, 2005). Figures published by the National Institute for Health and Clinical Excellence (NICE) state that:

> It has been estimated that approximately 1% of school-aged children (about 69,000 6–16 year olds in England and 4,200 in Wales) meet the diagnostic criteria for HKD (i.e. severe combined-type ADHD). The estimated prevalence of all ADHD is considerably higher, around 5% of school-aged children (345,000 in England and 21,000 in Wales). (2000: 3)

On average, this means that in a mainstream class of 30 children it is likely that at least one child will have ADHD. Distribution is not even, with some schools having a disproportionate number of students displaying ADHD-type characteristics. The average local prevalence rate in several local authorities where school surveys have been carried out was found to be approximately 0.5 per cent of each school population (Wheeler, 2007). In 151 out of 256 schools that responded to the ADHD survey there were 413 individuals reported as being formally diagnosed with ADHD. This represents 0.53 per cent of the total school population, i.e. 5.3 students per 1,000. It can be seen in the breakdown by age shown in Figure 1.3 that the highest proportion of diagnosed students was in the 7–11 years age group – this concurs with suggestions that the disorder is considered to be more prevalent in the age range 6–11 years with a reduction in prevalence with socio-emotional maturation.

Estimates of gender differences vary. Boys generally tend to outnumber girls, although there is a possibility of an under-representation of girls in estimated figures. It is believed that boys are more likely to be identified because they are likely to be more overtly aggressive and therefore to be noticed to have difficulties. Male-to-female ratios range from 4:1 to 9:1, depending on the setting (i.e. general population or clinics) (APA, 2000). These estimates depend significantly on which ADHD subtypes are included. Boys may outnumber girls by 4:1 in the hyperactive–impulsive/mixed type groups, but boys and girls are represented in about equal numbers in the

Age	Number of students	Percentage
4–5 years	17	4%
5–7 years	50	12%
7–11 years	152	37%
11–14 years	129	31%
14–16 years	54	13%
17–19 years	0	0
Not known	11	3%
Total	**413**	**100%**

Figure 1.3   Diagnosed ADHD students by age

non-hyperactive (mainly inattentive) type (Cooper and O'Regan, 2001). The school survey findings showed a boy:girl ratio of 9:1.

Coexisting problems

Most studies suggest that approximately 60 to 70 per cent of children and young people with ADHD have comorbid or coexisting conditions of various types. These coexisting conditions may add to the significant social, emotional and educational problems experienced by a child with ADHD. They may include disruptive behaviour disorders such as oppositional defiant disorder (ODD) and conduct disorder (CD); learning difficulties, dyslexia, speech and language disorders, dyspraxia and dyscalculia; depression and anxiety; obsessive compulsive disorder (OCD), tics and Tourette's syndrome. There are also suggestions of comorbidity with autistic spectrum disorders (ASD) including Asperger's syndrome. Other problems common in children with ADHD include poor self-esteem; fine motor control and handwriting difficulties; self-regulation of emotion; sense of time, time management and organisational problems; sleep difficulties; over-sensitivity; and problems with relationships. Over 50 per cent of children with ADHD display emotional problems and the same number display social skills problems (Cooper and Bilton, 2002).

In the school survey 70 per cent of diagnosed students were reported as having other special educational needs (SEN). Responses to the question regarding the description of other SEN confirm that there is evidence of comorbidity in individuals with ADHD, and in some cases multiple comorbidity. The highest number of students experienced emotional and behavioural difficulties (EBD), with the second highest proportion reported as experiencing general learning difficulties. Coexisting difficulties, including those experienced by the six target students in the case study research, fall into three categories: *cognitive difficulties* which may impede learning; *affective difficulties* which are more concerned with social, emotional and behavioural problems; and *other difficulties*. These are discussed in greater detail in Chapter 7.

Prognosis

Individuals with ADHD may experience difficulties with the transition from primary to secondary school, with increased emphasis placed on their abilities to be self-organised and autonomous, both in their learning and social behaviour. They may also have problems with the narrowing of the curriculum in the secondary school setting where more use is made of abstract and analytical learning approaches (BPS, 2000). Those students who display ADHD characteristics may be more likely than their non-ADHD peers to be excluded from school for behaviour reasons (Cooper and O'Regan, 2001).

For many years it was assumed that ADHD disappears at puberty and that children with ADHD would 'outgrow' behaviour difficulties associated with the disorder upon reaching adolescence or early adulthood. Longitudinal investigations show that 70 to 80 per cent of children continue to exhibit significant deficits in attention and impulsivity compared to their adolescent peers (DuPaul and Stoner, 2003). There is a need for more individualised treatments to take account of differing characteristics displayed by adolescents. Diagnosing ADHD in the teenage years is difficult because the core symptoms are often overshadowed by other coexisting conditions such as ODD and CD. Teenagers are often unwilling to cooperate with management strategies including medication (Kewley, 2005).

There are suggestions that between 30 and 70 per cent of those who have been diagnosed in childhood carry some or all of the ADHD traits into adulthood (Cooper, 2006), although the majority no longer meet the formal DSM diagnosis criteria for the disorder. The frequency and intensity of their symptoms decline. There is a lessening of impulsive behaviours, although the learning and organisational problems may persist. Green and Chee (1997) claim that adult ADHD was first recognised when paediatricians became aware that some of the parents of children in their care had the same symptoms as their children. Those in whom the condition persists into adulthood are likely to suffer from anti-social, self-destructive tendencies and experience difficulties with emotional and social problems, unemployment, criminality and substance abuse, other mental illnesses and increased accident rates. Only a few specialist clinics for adults with ADHD currently exist. If their ADHD is adequately treated, it should be possible for them to find a career and lifestyle in which they flourish. Features of ADHD such as creativity and high energy levels can be advantageous in adult working life.

Interventions

The heterogeneity in characteristics and symptoms displayed by students diagnosed with ADHD and the variability of their response to treatment means that it is often difficult to decide on the most effective interventions for each individual. There are several types of intervention currently used to treat individuals with ADHD who may experience difficulties in both the cognitive and affective domains. 'Research … indicates that a multimodal treatment protocol is more effective than unimodal treatment in addressing the myriad of difficulties associated with this disorder' (DuPaul and Weyandt, 2006: 342).

Medical interventions

Stimulant medications have been found to have positive effects on attention span, impulse control, academic performance and social relationships. By affecting the balance of noradrenaline and dopamine in the brain, the aim of medication is to control symptoms so that the child is more receptive to other forms of non-medical interventions. Medication '… can be seen to provide a "window of opportunity" for the child to benefit from teaching–learning experiences provided by teachers, parents and others' (Alban-Metcalfe and Alban-Metcalfe, 2001: 89). Chapter 2 provides a more comprehensive discussion regarding the use of medication in managing ADHD.

Educational interventions

Many of the educational and environmental interventions and classroom management strategies already in place in some schools may be differentially appropriate for students who display ADHD characteristics. There have been specific suggestions for classroom strategies for use with students diagnosed with ADHD. Some of these are identified in the references at the end of this book. One of the most important features is the 'need for curriculum implementation and organizational arrangements that are more geared to pupil learning styles' (Cooper, 2005: 133). Educational interventions specifically aimed at adolescents may need to focus more on homework, organisation, test preparation and test taking, note taking, reading comprehension, memorising, classroom participation and conduct (Robin, 1998). The findings from the case study research have identified settings and contexts which may lead to higher attainment in students with ADHD. The focus in Section 2 of this book is on the identification of interventions and strategies for use in the classroom.

Physical exercise in school
There have been suggestions that physical exercise increases dopamine levels in the brain, thus having a similar effect to that achieved by the taking of stimulant medication (Ratey, 2004). In a recent study, the 'on-task' behaviour of students with EBD in a mainstream secondary school showed improvements following Physical Education (PE) lessons (Medcalf et al., 2006). The inclusion of periods of structured physical activity at regular intervals throughout the school day could produce positive outcomes for students with ADHD (Cooper, 2005).

Nurture groups
Recently in some local authorities nurture groups have been set up in mainstream schools as an early intervention for children with social and emotional difficulties (Bennathan and Boxall, 2000). There is evidence that some individuals with ADHD may benefit from this type of setting, which combines the features of a caring, homely environment with those of a standard classroom and where the emphasis is on emotionally supportive and empathic relationships between adults and children. There is a predictable daily routine, which includes a holistic curriculum, intensive interaction, free play periods and periods of structured physical activity (Cooper, 2004). A typical nurture group consists of 10–12 students, a teacher and a teaching assistant. The students remain on the roll of a mainstream class, spending curriculum time in this class when not attending the nurture group. The students are usually reintegrated full-time into their mainstream classes after a period of between two and four terms.

Social interventions

Children and young people with ADHD often have poor social skills, finding difficulty in initiating and maintaining friendships. They appear unaware of how their behaviour affects other people and may, for example, try to join in a game without asking permission. They do not follow the rules of good conversation, are likely to interrupt others and are more likely than their non-ADHD peers to react aggressively. Consequently they may suffer from peer-rejection or isolation (DuPaul and Stoner, 2003). There is a need for the teaching of basic social interaction skills to individuals with ADHD. This may be accomplished at home by parents, in school and through voluntary agencies. Antshel (2005) suggests pre-school training in social skills for students with ADHD alongside typically developing peers in order to help foster improved social functioning from an early age.

Alternative/complementary interventions

Alternative and complementary treatments are often used in children with ADHD, but reported effectiveness is variable. Many interventions are controversial, have minimal or no established efficacy for children with ADHD and lack sufficient research evidence (DuPaul and Stoner, 2003). There is not room here to discuss the relative merits or otherwise of suggested treatments. The following list has been compiled with reference to several sources, some of which are listed in the suggestions for further reading:

- amino acid supplementation;

- brain gym;

- chiropractics;

- cognitive behaviour therapy;

- developmental optometry – eye exercises;

- diet – includes the adverse effects of food additives, food intolerance, deficiencies, allergies, the Feingold diet and dietary supplements, including fish oil;

- herbal or natural medicines;

- holistic approaches including acupuncture, aromatherapy, colour therapy, homeopathy, osteopathy, reflexology;

- multivitamins and zinc;

- play therapy and outdoor play in green places;

- tinted lenses;

- yoga.

Points to remember

- Diagnosis of ADHD is made by a medical clinician.
- ADHD is not a modern disorder.
- There is no one single 'cause' of ADHD. It is considered to be a bio-psycho-social disorder.
- It is estimated that between 1 and 5 per cent of school-aged children in the UK may have ADHD.
- Approximately 60 to 70 per cent of children with ADHD have comorbid or coexisting conditions of various types.
- ADHD is not simply a childhood disorder. It can persist into adulthood in some form or another.
- A multi-modal, multi-professional treatment approach should include a combination of medical, psychological, social and educational interventions.

Questions for reflection and discussion

1. What specifically are you hoping to learn from reading this book?
2. Have you or any members of your school received any training in ADHD?
3. Do you believe a diagnosis of ADHD is a help or a hindrance:

   (a) to the student?
   (b) to the parents?
   (c) to the school?

4. If 1–5 per cent of students have ADHD how many in your school or class are likely to have it?
5. What aspects of schools might present difficulties for students with ADHD?

 Remember: 'Myth or Fact?' sheets (Figures 1.1 and 1.2) are also available from www.sagepub.co.uk/wheeler

2

Use of medication

Although this book is written from an educational perspective with the main focus on school interventions and strategies, it is important that all educational practitioners have some basic understanding of the use of medication in the management of ADHD, as this is one of the most controversial issues surrounding the disorder. This chapter will help to raise your awareness of medical interventions, beginning with details of the different types of medication available. The numbers of students prescribed medication and the reported effectiveness of medical intervention are discussed. Finally, differing viewpoints concerning the use of medication are examined.

When medication is used it should be as part of a multi-modal, multi-professional treatment approach. Medical intervention is not necessary in all cases of ADHD. Some individuals with milder symptoms might benefit from non-pharmacological interventions which combine educational, psychological and social approaches. These approaches may also be used in cases where parents and/or students are reluctant to use medication. In each case, the decision about whether to prescribe medication or not should be made by the clinician in collaboration with the child or young person concerned and his or her parents or carers (NICE, 2008), following an initial referral often from a GP.

Types and use of medication

Psychostimulant medications such as methylphenidate (Ritalin, Equasym) and dexamphetamine (Dexedrine, Adderall) are used to increase the arousal of the central nervous system. In simple terms medication allows 'actions and thought processes to take place smoothly, without being blocked and without digression and side-tracking' (Kewley, 2005: 45). The original forms of psychostimulant are short-acting and administered two or three times daily. Sustained release versions such as Concerta are now available and are becoming the preferred form for treating most children with ADHD. These once-daily formulations are beneficial as they do not require mid-day doses to be administered at school. There is evidence for the effectiveness of psychostimulants in pre-school children. Dexamphetamine is licensed for use in patients aged 3 years or above (SIGN, 2001). Methylphenidate has traditionally been the most commonly used medication in the treatment of ADHD. It is licensed for use in children aged 6 years and above, although its use in younger children has caused considerable debate. In the case study research, David and Edward were prescribed Ritalin before the age of 6 years.

Following a comprehensive evaluation, the clinician will probably start by prescribing a low dose of the short-acting medication, usually Ritalin, gradually increasing in multiples of 5 mg until the dose that gives maximum advantage without side effects is found. Very young children may need to start on quarter-tablet doses. Tablets can be taken with or without food. The maximum dose that is recommended in the UK is 60 mg in a 24-hour period. Most children do not need that much. Once the correct dosage has been found, medication should help the core ADHD symptoms within about 20 minutes. It will reach its highest concentration in the brain within one or two hours and will cease to act after about four or five hours. The dose and timing for each individual usually stays the same over the years, although with age and puberty there is sometimes a need for an increase in dosage. Some adjustment may be needed on entry to secondary school where there are longer school days and more homework demands. If there is no improvement in the child's symptoms with one type of medication, an alternative may be used. If there is still no improvement, the use of medication should be discontinued and the diagnosis reviewed. In some cases, particularly if there are comorbid disorders, combined drug treatments may be used.

Psychostimulant medications are controlled drugs and should be kept securely in the home and school. An adult should be responsible for supervising their use, although children should be encouraged to become involved in remembering when the next dose is due. More responsible teenagers may be allowed to take more control over the taking of their medication. If a mid-day dose is required at school it is important that the individual is able to take medication without being bullied or teased. Teaching staff should be supportive and develop a routine that does not draw attention to the student who may have to report to the school secretary's office at lunchtime (Kewley, 2005).

There is some evidence of misuse of ADHD medication, in particular Ritalin:

- *As a recreational drug.* Some teenagers use it to achieve an amphetamine-like rush, similar to the 'high' experienced when using cocaine.

- *As a study aid.* It has been alleged that some parents are buying Ritalin to boost their children's performance during exam times. It enables youngsters to work late and focus the mind.

In 2004 in the US it was reported that about 2.5 per cent of 13–14 year olds and 5.1 per cent of 17–18 year olds have taken the drug illegally for one of the above purposes. There is anecdotal evidence in the UK of students selling their prescription medication or being targeted by bullies who steal it (Brettingham, 2007). In earlier research in the US, Moline and Frankenberger (2001) found that out of fifty students receiving medication who completed anonymous self-report questionnaires, 34 per cent reported being approached to trade or sell their medication.

Atomoxetine (Strattera) is a *non-stimulant* medication which was licensed for use in the US in 2002 and in the UK in 2004 to treat children aged 6 years and over, adolescents and adults. It is described as 'a selective noradrenaline reuptake inhibitor, although the precise mechanism by which it works on ADHD is unknown' (NICE, 2006: 8). It is long-acting, lasting generally for 24 hours, and is particularly effective for behavioural problems at the start and end of the day. As a non-stimulant, Strattera is not classed as a controlled drug. Initial symptom reduction may be seen in the first week, with near maximum symptom reduction achieved after approximately four weeks of treatment.

Other types of medication have been used successfully in treating ADHD. These include *tricyclic antidepressant medications* (TCAs) such as imipramine (Tofranil) and desipramine (Norpramine). 'Clinical trials have demonstrated the effectiveness of TCAs in the treatment of ADHD/HKD in children from nursery age to adolescence' (SIGN, 2001: 15). These are slower acting and are usually prescribed to children who either do not respond to stimulants or who have coexisting symptoms of anxiety or clinical depression.

Numbers of students prescribed medication

In the US, 90 per cent of children diagnosed with ADHD receive medication therapy. The vast majority, approximately 1.5 million children (more than 4 per cent of the school age population) are treated with psychostimulant medications (DuPaul and Stoner, 2003). In the UK, there are suggestions that the disorder is undertreated. It is estimated that between approximately 10 and 20 per cent of children with ADHD receive medication. The average duration of medication use is between two and seven years, although this will vary from case to case.

Of the 75 per cent of diagnosed individuals reported as being prescribed medication in the school survey, 88 per cent were known to be taking methylphenidate (Ritalin or Concerta). The use of slow-release drugs such as Concerta, which are taken once daily in the morning, is reflected in the figure of 56 per cent of students who take their medication at home. All four diagnosed boys in the case studies were prescribed Ritalin initially, with David's medication being changed to Concerta after approximately four years and Carl's after three years (Wheeler, 2007).

Reported effectiveness

'When used in conjunction with other strategies, the correct use of medication is one of the most effective forms of therapy in ADHD. Experienced ADHD clinics report an improvement in symptoms in 80–95 per cent of cases' (Kewley, 2005: 43). There are reports of improvements in classroom behaviour, attention and concentration in children with ADHD, although there have been conflicting results for the effects on academic achievement. Positive effects on peer and family relationships have been observed. High-school students in the US with ADHD reported improvements in social and behavioural areas and attention rather than academic achievement enhancement with the use of stimulant medication. They were unsure if the medication helped them when taking tests or doing homework (Moline and Frankenberger, 2001). Comments made by students aged 11–16 years in a study undertaken by Cooper and Shea (1999) reflected both positive and negative attitudes to medication. On the positive side medication is welcomed as it helps them to concentrate and leads to educational improvement. However, on the negative side the students express concern about the effects of medication on their spontaneity and sense of personal identity.

Positive behaviour changes with medication were reported by teaching staff in 70 per cent of cases in the school survey. Examples of these included: 'calmer', 'more focused', 'improved concentration', 'less aggressive' and 'less fidgety'. Little or no difference was identified in 10 per cent of cases. A small proportion of comments were phrased negatively, for example: 'less involved' and 'zombie-like'. It can be seen from the following case study extract that, after only a month on medication, the school was able to report some improvement in Adam's classroom behaviour.

 Case study

Adam – diagnosis and medication

Adam is the only target student to have been formally diagnosed with ADHD and prescribed Ritalin during the course of the case study research period. It was therefore possible to observe him in school settings before and after medication (see Chapter 4 for further details of observation findings). His Individual Education Plan (IEP) review approximately a month after diagnosis of ADHD reported:

- Since starting taking Ritalin has been quieter and less impulsive in school.
- Ability to concentrate and remain on task varies, but on the whole is improving.
- When reminded is able to wait his turn to answer questions.

Arguments for and against medication

The use of medication in the treatment of ADHD is one of the most contentious issues surrounding the disorder. As reported above, arguments in favour of medical intervention include reported positive effects on peer and family relationships as well as improvements in classroom behaviour, attention and concentration in children with ADHD.

Critics of medication cite various *side effects* that have been reported with its use. The most common short-term side effects include appetite suppression, abdominal pain, headaches, sleep difficulties, rebound effect, tics, itchy skin, rashes, a feeling of depression, mood change or nausea (Kewley, 2005). 'Side effects are relatively benign and are more likely to occur at higher dose levels' (DuPaul and Stoner, 2003: 222). Suggested long-term side effects are suppression of height and weight gain. Cooper and Bilton report that '... growth retardation is *not* a significant risk factor, although in some cases children under 10 years of age show a transient decrease in weight and slight growth slowing, which later normalise' (2002: 80). It is important that all medication effects, both positive and negative, are monitored closely.

Case study

David – medication side effects

During the first year of the case study it was reported that David, aged 9 years, had been experiencing a loss of appetite when taking medication. It was necessary for the school to work closely with David and his parents to offer support and to try to alleviate this. In the past his parents had tried taking him off medication for a while but this had an adverse effect on his behaviour.

The Special Educational Needs Coordinator (SENCO) first recommended changing the timing of his lunchtime tablet and the lunchtime supervisors were all made aware of the need to encourage him to eat more. When this made little difference, the SENCO suggested that David brought in sandwiches from home, thus providing an opportunity for him to have food of his own choice.

The following year David was prescribed Concerta, which meant that he only had to take one tablet at home in the morning. Although there had been some improvement, there were still worries about his appetite and by the end of the research period the SENCO had agreed to arrange to have the dosage reviewed.

Another argument put forward against the use of medication to treat ADHD is the *potential for drug abuse and addiction*. There is no evidence of addiction to stimulants used in the treatment of ADHD. 'Methylphenidate in particular is seen as an extremely safe medication, being non-addictive' (Cooper, 2006: 259).

There have also been concerns about *the involvement of large pharmaceutical companies* (a) offering financial incentives to parent support groups and (b) making huge profits through increasing numbers of prescriptions. It should be borne in mind that 'Extended-release stimulant and non-stimulant treatments for ADHD … would not have been possible without considerable investment on the part of the pharmaceutical industry' (Coghill, 2005: 288).

The *costs to health and other public services* are factors to be considered in the widespread use of medication to treat ADHD (NICE, 2006). Dexedrine is the cheapest option and for this reason is the most commonly used drug in Australia. The slow-release versions are the most expensive. 'One study estimated the excess cost of the condition (relating to education, occupation impairment and medical treatment) to be $31.6 billion in the USA in 2000' (Chamberlain and Sahakian, 2006: 35). In 1998 there were approximately 220,000 prescriptions for stimulant medications in England at a net cost of approximately £5 million. The number of prescriptions rose to 418,300 in 2004, at a cost of almost £13 million a year, with modified-release formulations of methylphenidate accounting for 54 per cent of all prescriptions. Guidance on the use of methylphenidate, atomoxetine and dexamfetamine suggests 'if there is a choice of more than one appropriate drug, the product with the lowest cost (taking into account the cost per dose and number of daily doses) should be prescribed' (NICE, 2006: 5).

There are *other implications for public spending* in addition to the costs of assessment, medication and follow-up discussed above. In the UK, families with a disabled child are entitled to claim Disability Living Allowance (DLA). As ADHD is a medical diagnosis, some parents are encouraged to apply for a weekly cash payment of DLA as a means of reducing the burden of ADHD at a family level. In 2002, when weekly amounts of DLA varied between £14.20 and £90.95, it was reported that 'even using the lower care component DLA rate of £14.20, the annual DLA cost could exceed £100 million as increasing proportions of children with a diagnosis of ADHD are included in treatment programmes' (Steyn et al., 2002: 524). In 2009 weekly amounts had increased to between £18.65 and £119.45.

A further area of debate focuses on the lack of *evaluation of long-term efficacy*. The longer-term effects of medication are far from clear and a legitimate field for further research. Very few studies have been carried out and most have been of short duration. Inconsistencies in findings 'may be attributable to failure to control for the type and severity of the ADHD, and/or for type and dosage of medication, and/or for the existence of other associated or comorbid conditions, and/or the type and quality of the accompanying educational interventions, if any' (Alban-Metcalfe and Alban-Metcalfe, 2001: 89).

Monitoring medication

It is important that the correct dose of medication is prescribed and that regular reviews take place to monitor dosage and timing and to consider any side effects. Effective cooperation between education and health professionals and parents is crucial in monitoring the positive and negative effects of medication (DuPaul and Stoner, 2003). This is discussed further in Chapter 3 which focuses on the importance of a multi-professional approach to identification, assessment and management of ADHD.

 Points to remember

- The aim of medication is to control ADHD symptoms so that the child is more receptive to other forms of non-medical interventions.
- The majority of students prescribed medication use methylphenidate (Ritalin or Concerta).
- Benefits can include improvements in classroom behaviour, attention and concentration as well as positive effects on peer and family relationships.
- There can be mild side effects such as loss of appetite, abdominal pain, headaches and sleep difficulties. These can generally be controlled by adjusting the dosage.
- When medication is used in the management of ADHD its use should be carefully monitored and utilised only as part of multi-modal treatment.

 Questions for reflection and discussion

1. How do you feel about the use of medication for students with ADHD?
2. Are there any difficulties in your school regarding the use of medication?
3. Have any improvements in behaviour been noted with students with ADHD using medication as part of a multi-modal intervention?

3

Multi-professional involvements

This final chapter in Section 1 focuses in detail on multi-professional and multi-disciplinary approaches in the identification, assessment and management of ADHD. Several issues are discussed, including:

- the need for effective liaison between health and educational professionals, particularly when medication is used as part of a multi-modal intervention;
- multi-professional care pathways;
- the involvement of parents and schools in identification and assessment procedures;
- differences in awareness and attitudes among professionals and parents; and
- the use of labels or diagnostic classifications such as ADHD.

A multi-professional approach

An accurate assessment of ADHD requires evidence of pervasiveness and should be based on detailed information from parents, teachers, educational psychologists and other professionals, with the formal diagnosis being made by a medical clinician. As previously mentioned, where medication is included as part of a multi-modal management approach, it is essential that all concerned parties are involved in monitoring the effects of medication, both positive and negative, and that regular reviews take place.

Professionals from different disciplines need to agree on a set of common assumptions in order to ensure effective multi-professional working. Guidelines have been drawn up for the management of ADHD, but any inter-professional collaboration may present difficulties. Professionals working together in delivering services for a condition like ADHD may have competing professional, political and economic agendas (Hughes and Cooper, 2007). There can be practical as well as theoretical problems in a multi-professional approach. Research carried out recently in Scotland among professionals who work with children in a variety of settings reported a 'lack of clarity about role boundaries, routes of referral and sources of advice and support for teachers' (Connelly et al., 2008: 16). Education professionals have traditionally been subject to legislation and guidance from the relevant government departments, including those focusing on SEN provision. Medical professionals work within health legislation and are required to take account of National Health Service (NHS) guidelines, including those published by the National Institute for Health and Clinical Excellence (NICE). There have been calls for closer working between professions in order to meet the needs of children more effectively and it has been suggested that a 'lead professional' or single named professional be identified to ensure a coherent package of services in cases where children and young people are supported by more than one specialist agency (DfES, 2003).

Variability in multi-professional working

Information gathered in the case study research indicating a shortage of child psychiatrists concurs with suggestions of variable access to child and adolescent mental health services, leading to long waiting lists for assessment for ADHD (NICE, 2000). The National Child and Adolescent Mental Health Services (CAMHS) Review (2008) has also reported wide variation in multi-agency provision for the mental health and well-being of children and young people and their families. The findings from the author's research suggest that there can be variability in multi-professional working in the identification and management of ADHD in different local authorities and also in schools within the same local authority. Only 23 per cent of schools had been asked to complete a questionnaire or behaviour rating list prior to diagnosis being made by a clinician. Following diagnosis, only 8 per cent of schools reported having been asked to fill in a questionnaire by a clinician.

In the school survey educational professionals were asked to provide information on the numbers of students with a clinical diagnosis of ADHD. The findings suggest that schools do not always have accurate information regarding diagnosis of the disorder, in some cases relying on parents to provide details. Multiple responses were recorded on some questionnaires to the question regarding diagnosis by different agencies, possibly pointing to a lack of knowledge on the part of school staff as to who makes the diagnosis. The highest numbers of ADHD diagnoses were reportedly made by paediatricians (33 per cent), with psychiatrists reported as diagnosing 21 per cent.

Multi-professional care pathways

There is not simply one correct way of dealing with the assessment and management of ADHD and there is a possibility of a wide variation in referral and care pathways in different areas. Some local authorities or health services may provide details of suggested ADHD care pathways following agreements with all of the agencies involved. Figure 3.1 offers an example of a basic care pathway model. The NICE guidance offers recommendations for a more comprehensive care pathway for the treatment and care of people with ADHD. This includes sections on:

- identification and referral of children and young people with ADHD;

- identification and referral of adults with ADHD;

- diagnosis of ADHD;

- post-diagnostic advice;

- treatment for children and young people with ADHD and moderate impairment;

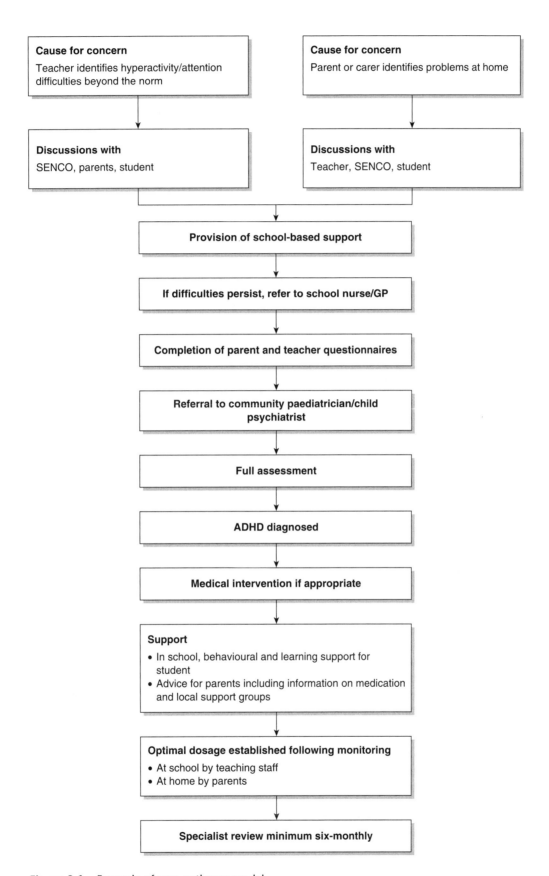

Figure 3.1 Example of care pathway model

- treatment for children and young people with severe ADHD and severe impairment;

- pre-drug treatment assessment;

- choice of drug for children and young people with ADHD;

- poor response to treatment;

- transition to adult services;

- treatment of adults with ADHD. (NICE, 2008)

Parental and school involvement

Although ADHD is a medical disorder, an initial concern leading to a referral to a clinician can come from several sources, including parents, teachers, SENCOs, educational psychologists, GPs, social services, local support groups or other interested parties. Of the four target students who had received a formal diagnosis of ADHD by the end of the case study research period, schools had been directly involved in the initial referral for assessment in the cases of Carl and Adam. For David and Edward the initial referral came from health service professionals and the schools were informed by the parents of their child's ADHD diagnosis.

Parental involvement

Parents may choose to approach the school or a GP in the first instance if they have any concerns about their child. Information from parents or carers during the assessment process is crucial. They are best placed to provide details of the child's early development, medical problems, behaviour patterns, dietary and sleep habits, abilities and interactions with siblings and peers (Cooper and Bilton, 2002). Where medication is used as part of a multi-modal intervention, parents are also in the best position to monitor the effects of medication on their child in the home situation. Chapter 8 offers a more comprehensive description of parental involvement and the importance of effective home–school relationships.

School involvement

'After parents, teachers are the people most of us spend most of our time with between the ages of 5 and 16' (Hughes and Cooper, 2007: 70). When the child starts school, daily interactions provide opportunities for teachers to observe the child or young person in educational settings over a sustained period of time and to build up a picture of the child's strengths and difficulties in academic, social and behavioural areas. Teachers are in the best position to compare the child's academic progress and behaviour with his or her peers (Cooper and Bilton, 2002). They can also play an important role in monitoring the positive and negative effects of medication and other interventions in the school setting (see examples from case studies in Chapter 2). The SEN identification and assessment procedure adopted by schools can be a useful framework within which ADHD assessment can take place. The evidence gathered by schools seeking additional support for a student's learning or behaviour difficulties can contribute in some cases to an eventual diagnosis of ADHD, as in the case of Adam (see Chapter 8).

Many of the diagnosed students recorded in the school survey experienced a range of comorbid or associated conditions and would require support from several agencies. All six target students in the case study research had reached the stage where external agencies had become involved in addressing their learning and behavioural needs. The numbers of extra professionals involved in supporting these individuals ranged from 4 to 16.

 Case study

Carl – multi-professional involvement

Carl had been placed on the SEN register on entry to primary school as he clearly experienced problems with learning, motor control and behaviour. As he progressed through the SEN and ADHD assessment procedures, he received extra support from the following agencies and professionals:

School:

1. SENCO
2. Teaching assistants
3. Special support assistant (SSA) providing 7.5 hours per week individual support (in his final year at primary school)

Local authority:

4. Educational psychology service
5. Learning and behaviour support service
6. Specific learning difficulties centre
7. Statementing officer

Specialist children's services (health services):

8. Clinical psychologist
9. Communication and social behaviour assessment team
10. Community paediatrician
11. Consultant child psychiatrist
12. Consultant community paediatrician
13. General practitioner
14. Paediatric occupational therapist
15. Physiotherapist
16. Speech and language therapist

Carl received a diagnosis of ADHD at age 6 years 9 months and showed some initial improvement in his behaviour following the prescription of medication. The following year it was reported at a review that: *'despite considerable input from several agencies, he has not made any significant progress. Move for statutory assessment'.* Over two years later a Statement of SEN was issued. This focused on his learning difficulties.

Although there is clear evidence of a multi-agency approach to the identification and assessment of SEN and the diagnosis and management of ADHD, this does not necessarily mean that Carl received more support or better provision than other students. There is even a possibility that a large number of involved professionals could sometimes be counter-productive. Even though he had shown cause for concern on entering primary school, it was not until his final year that a Statement of SEN was issued (Wheeler, 2007).

Differences in attitudes and awareness

Differences in attitudes and awareness of schools and parents to the concept of ADHD may have contributed to variability in the reported prevalence of ADHD and in identification and assessment procedures in the schools included in the research. Findings from the school survey show that only 59 per cent of schools (151 out of 256 who responded) reported students on roll with a formal ADHD diagnosis. A total of 92 schools (36 per cent of those who responded) reported at least one other student on roll who might have ADHD. This could indicate an underestimate of actual prevalence. Of the schools involved in the case study research, Carl's school (with approximately 440 students on roll) reported eight students diagnosed with ADHD. Three schools (including Sanjay's and Adam's schools, both with over 400 on roll) reported no students diagnosed with ADHD. This was despite indications that in each mainstream class at least one student may have ADHD (Cooper and Bilton, 2002).

 Case study

Sanjay – attitudes to ADHD diagnosis

At the beginning of the case study Sanjay was 7 years old. Two years previously the SENCO had suggested to his parents that he displayed many ADHD-type characteristics. They were reluctant to consider ADHD and, as the school adopted an inclusive policy and sought to support students without necessarily having recourse to 'labels', an assessment was not pursued. In addition to teachers and classroom assistants, the following were involved in supporting Sanjay:

School:

1. SENCO
2. SEN teacher
3. Teaching assistants

Local authority:

4. Learning and Behaviour Support Service (LBSS)

Specialist children's services (health services):

5. School nurse

By the end of the second year of the case study the SENCO reported, *'Sanjay's behaviour is becoming more difficult to control.'* He was due to move to a large middle school and there were concerns among first-school staff that he might not receive as much individual support as he had done previously.

Sanjay's case study highlights difficulties which may occur due to parental reluctance to consider an assessment for ADHD and also differences in attitudes between schools. Sanjay's first school (described by school inspectors as 'a truly inclusive school') adopted a nurturing, supportive attitude to its students and did not try to persuade Sanjay's parents to consider an ADHD diagnosis. The middle school would probably be operated more along the lines of a secondary school where students are expected to be more organised and independent. Sanjay had been used to receiving plenty of extra school-based support. Without more involvement from other agencies, possibly including assessment for ADHD, his learning and behaviour difficulties could become more difficult to support in a middle school setting.

 Case study

Fergal – attitudes to ADHD diagnosis

When he was aged 7 years Fergal had attended a local pupil referral unit (PRU) for three days a week and mainstream school for two days. A Statement of SEN had been issued two years later to support his complex range of learning difficulties and challenging behaviours. Fergal had been identified to the researcher by an educational psychologist as displaying many of the characteristics associated with ADHD. Systematic observations during the case study confirmed this. He received additional support from the following:

School:

1. SENCO
2. Teaching assistants
3. Special support assistant (SSA) offering individual support
4. Nurture group staff

Local authority:

5. Educational Psychology Service
6. Learning and Behaviour Support Service (LBSS)
7. Pupil referral unit (PRU)
8. Statementing officer

Specialist children's services (health services):

9. Community paediatrician
10. Speech and language therapist.

(Continued)

> *(Continued)*
>
> However, by the end of the research period Fergal had not been put forward for formal assessment of ADHD. In an interview with the researcher at the beginning of the research period, the head teacher/SENCO of Fergal's first school stated: *'Our parents are not the sort that go for getting labels like ADHD for their children.'*

Fergal's first-school ethos was similar to that of Sanjay's school, although from the SENCO's comments, it is not known if any definite approach had been made to his parents regarding the possibility of ADHD assessment. During the first year of the case study Fergal attended mainstream school on a full-time basis and benefited from spending four mornings per week in a nurture group which had recently been introduced in the school. He remained on the main class register and joined his peers for the rest of the week, often with individual SSA support. The following year when he moved to middle school it was felt necessary for him to attend another PRU on a part-time basis. Following the research period there was a suggestion that he might have to attend the PRU full-time as staff in the mainstream school were finding it increasingly difficult to offer him the support he needed.

A lack of awareness or ineffective multi-disciplinary cooperation in identification and treatment could lead to underdiagnosis (Alban-Metcalfe and Alban-Metcalfe, 2001) or undertreatment of ADHD. If untreated the disorder may interfere with educational and social development and predispose to psychiatric and other difficulties. Untreated ADHD could also lead to exclusion from mainstream education, conduct disorder in adolescence, delinquency and crime and substance abuse in later life (Kewley, 2005). It was recently reported that 'underdiagnosis of ADHD is an issue in Scotland – it is likely that there are at least 7,000 children and young people with ADHD not getting the support that they need' (NHS Quality Improvement Scotland, 2008: 10).

The perceptions and knowledge of teachers and parents and their attitudes towards ADHD could have implications for the delivery of suitable educational provision for individuals with the disorder. If multi-professional approaches to identification and management of ADHD are to be effective it is necessary for educational professionals to be provided with opportunities to increase their knowledge and expertise in managing all types of SEN, including ADHD, in the school situation. There has been no specific mention of ADHD in government guidance to date, although the SEN strategy states, 'We want to see all teachers having the skills and confidence – and access to specialist advice where necessary – to help children with SEN to reach their potential' (DfES, 2004: 50).

The last two items on the school survey questionnaire specifically referred to relevant school training. Staff in 12 per cent (N = 31) of the schools that responded to this question indicated that they had received some training in ADHD. Invited to tick as many boxes as appropriate, of the 211 responses to the question: *What kind of training would be most useful?*

- 36 per cent (N = 76) requested an information pack;

- 34 per cent (N = 72) asked for a twilight session;

- 16 per cent (N = 34) were interested in a whole day's training; and

- 14 per cent (N = 29) asked for a support group.

Although the findings from the research suggest some increase in awareness of ADHD among teachers, the response in the ADHD survey, together with feedback from delegates at two ADHD study days held at a university during the research period, clearly underlines the need for more training, information, research and proactive strategies to be made available to schools (Wheeler, 2007). (Further details regarding the ADHD study days are included in Chapter 5.)

Diagnostic classifications and labelling

The cases of Sanjay and Fergal, described above, highlight an important area of debate in the management of ADHD, that of varying attitudes to diagnostic classifications and 'labelling' of children and young people. One of the main criticisms regarding the use of diagnostic criteria checklists is that they rely on subjective judgements with regard to frequency of behaviours (BPS, 1996). The ICD-10 criteria use words such as 'unduly', 'excessive', 'markedly' and 'significant'. In 16 out of 18 DSM-IV criteria the word 'often' is used. Limitations of a categorical approach include the heterogeneity of symptoms displayed by individuals sharing a diagnosis and the need for experienced clinical judgement in making a diagnosis (APA, 2000).

The issue of 'labels' often focuses on the relationships between the professions involved in treating students who have the disorder. Educational legislation in the UK does not require categories of disability in order to provide for individuals with special educational needs. The medical profession requires diagnostic criteria or classification particularly if it includes prescription (BPS, 1996). Labels can be used in negative or positive ways and some inclusive schools reject using labels just for the sake of them. Those from various professions who view labels such as ADHD as constructive emphasise their use in accessing the required support for the student. Others focus on the necessity of a label or diagnosis in order for families of children with ADHD to obtain extra financial support. The important factor is that labels should be used consistently across disciplines. They should 'provide a picture of the child's functional deficits and result in a more complete understanding of how to support different children with their different patterns of difficulty' (Kirby et al., 2005: 126).

The three chapters in Section 1 have provided background information on the concept of ADHD including the controversial nature of the disorder, the use of medication as an intervention and, in this chapter, the importance of effective multi-professional cooperation. Section 2 will focus on the school setting, beginning in Chapter 4 by discussing systematic classroom observation.

Points to remember

- It is essential that a multi-professional approach is adopted in the identification, assessment and management of ADHD.
- There is variability in effective multi-professional working and variable access to child and adolescent mental health services.
- The SEN identification and assessment procedure adopted by schools can be a useful framework within which ADHD assessment can take place.
- Differences in attitudes and awareness may contribute to underestimates of prevalence.
- There is a need for increasing the awareness and knowledge of ADHD among parents and all professionals involved in the identification and diagnosis of the disorder.

Questions for reflection and discussion

1. What information from other professionals would you find useful in teaching students with ADHD?
2. What information can your school provide to other professionals that would help in the assessment and management of the disorder?
3. Have you or the school experienced any difficulties in working with professionals from other disciplines? How could these be avoided?

Section 2

The School Setting

4

Systematic classroom observation

> Section 2 focuses on the school setting. This chapter begins with a discussion of the importance of detailed observation of individual students in educational contexts. Full details of two new systematic classroom observation schedules devised by the author are presented. Extracts from case studies illustrate three practical applications of the observation techniques:
>
> - to facilitate the gathering of practice-based evidence in assessment processes;
> - to help in monitoring the effects of medication or other interventions; and
> - to identify contextual and curricular settings and approaches which may help teachers to enhance on-task behaviour.

Systematic observation

Teachers and other educational professionals are aware of the importance of observing students who may be showing cause for concern, with the possibility of learning and/or behavioural difficulties connected with ADHD. In many cases initial informal observation or general behaviour checklists may be useful, but there are circumstances when there is a need for more systematic direct observation. Data collected using systematic techniques can have practical applications in investigating and quantifying the ADHD and non-ADHD behaviour of learners of all ages in all types of educational settings. It is important to be aware of the uniqueness of individual students who display ADHD characteristics. Because of variability in ADHD behaviours, both within-child and across cases, it is essential that observations are undertaken across settings and over time.

The use of systematic observation techniques has the benefit of minimising observer bias as well as confirming informal teacher evaluations of student behaviour. There are many examples of published ADHD schedules and rating scales for observation of classroom behaviour which use interval or time sampling methods of recording in evaluations of school functioning. Some focus on the three core ADHD symptoms displayed by a target student (Daniel and Cooper, 1999). Others also observe the behaviour of a comparison same-sex student (Lovey, 1999). In the author's research the intention was to monitor individual students over time and to record accurately the numbers of specific ADHD behaviours they displayed over given periods. The published observation schedules available at the time were not considered suitable in their original form for use in the case study research and so a decision was made to modify existing instruments in order to gather appropriate quantitative classroom data on the variability of ADHD symptoms. The two schedules were developed from this theoretical perspective.

DuPaul and Stoner recommend two goals for the school-based direct observation stage of the multi-method assessment of ADHD: '(1) to establish the frequency of inattentive, impulsive and/or restless behaviours relative to classmates; and (2) to obtain stable unbiased estimates of these frequencies by conducting observations on several occasions in the same classroom setting' (2003: 41). Bearing these suggestions in mind, it was decided by the author that for the case studies two different time sampling techniques were required to collate sufficient data on variability across curricular contexts, over time and between students with and without ADHD:

1. a schedule which would enable data to be collected on both the target student and a non-ADHD peer for purposes of comparison (later referred to as instantaneous time sampling or ITS);

2. a schedule which would provide data regarding frequency and duration of ADHD and non-ADHD behaviours, focusing on the target student (later referred to as fixed interval sampling or FIS).

Instantaneous time sampling (ITS)

In instantaneous time sampling the observer codes what is happening at particular predetermined moments in time rather than recording retrospectively what has occurred during a time period (as in FIS observation – see below). It is important that the class teacher identifies a same-sex classmate as 'typical' or 'average' as a comparison, as the classroom level of acceptable behaviour can vary depending on a particular teacher's expectation and tolerance. By recording 'snapshots' of behaviour at particular instants for both the case study individual (target student) and the non-ADHD (comparison) student over fixed time periods, the observer is able to gather comparative quantitative data on the target student's behaviour as related to other students. This technique also enables quantitative comparison over time, so that improvement or decline can be recorded (Cooper and O'Regan, 2001).

Dr Sam Goldstein first introduced the 'TOAD' system to collect data on four classroom behaviours that are frequently problematic for learners with ADHD. The four behaviours are 'Talking out', 'Out of seat', 'Attention problems' and 'Disruption' (Goldstein and Goldstein, 1998). A later adaptation by Lovey (1999) enabled further comparisons to be made between a child suspected of displaying ADHD characteristics and a non-ADHD child. Both students were observed and the behaviours were recorded every 30 seconds for 10 minutes in three lessons using a simple sheet. Lessons involving different demands and settings were chosen, for example English, maths and science or technology. It was usually possible to ascertain whether the target student displayed notably more of the four behaviours than a classmate chosen as a control or comparison.

Instantaneous Time Sampling

Behaviour according to DSM-IV criteria

Inattention

1. Fails to give close attention to details
2. Difficulty sustaining attention
3. Does not appear to listen
4. Difficulty in following through instructions
5. Avoids tasks requiring sustained mental effort
6. Difficulty in organising tasks and activities
7. Loses things necessary for tasks and activities
8. Easily distracted by extraneous stimuli
9. Forgetful

Hyperactivity

10. Fidgets with hands or feet or squirms in seat
11. Unauthorised movement in the classroom
12. Runs about or climbs excessively in situations where it is inappropriate
13. Has difficulty in playing quietly
14. Is often 'on the go'
15. Talks excessively

Impulsiveness

16. Blurts out answers
17. Difficulty awaiting turn
18. Interrupts or intrudes upon others (butts in)

0. None of the above behaviours

Date	Time	Context:

Recordings of observations of target student and comparison behaviours taken at 30-second intervals for a 10-minute period

T																				
	1	2	3	4	5	6	7	8	9	10	11	12	13	14	15	16	17	18	19	20
C																				

T																				
	1	2	3	4	5	6	7	8	9	10	11	12	13	14	15	16	17	18	19	20
C																				

T																				
	1	2	3	4	5	6	7	8	9	10	11	12	13	14	15	16	17	18	19	20
C																				

Analysis

Time	Context	Target:			Comparison:		
		No ADHD	Inattention	Hyp/Imp	No ADHD	Inattention	Hyp/Imp
Totals							
Percentages							

 Figure 4.1   Instantaneous time sampling observation schedule

Instantaneous Time Sampling – Instructions

Purpose

- ITS is used to gather quantitative data regarding how many times ADHD behaviours are recorded during a 10-minute time period (frequency).

- It may be used for comparison between behaviours displayed by the target (T) and comparison student (C) (a non-ADHD peer previously nominated by the class teacher).

- This type of recording can be used for 1, 2 or 3 × 10-minute periods (or even more), or for part of a 10-minute period, for example during an assembly which lasts 25 minutes recordings could be taken throughout.

Description of instrument

- The ITS schedule includes a table listing all 18 ADHD DSM-IV criteria, subdivided into the three core behaviour categories.

- There are three recording boxes on the sheet each consisting of a 10-minute time line with 20 cells for behaviour recordings for both the target student and the comparison student at 30-second intervals.

- The analysis section is divided into three behaviour columns for both the target and comparison students.

Procedure

- Familiarise yourself with DSM-IV criteria for ADHD.

- Remain as unobtrusive as possible and ideally take no part in the lesson.

- Record on the sheet: the name of the target student and comparison; the date and time; brief details regarding context and setting, including the number in the group (i.e. class group, whole school, etc.) and if there is just a teacher or whether any support is given (e.g. TA offering general support or SSA supporting one particular child).

- If planning to use 3 × 10-minute periods in a lesson (start, middle and end) it is helpful to know the approximate time the lesson will end. If a lesson is timed for an hour it is relatively easy to spread out the three 10-minute recording periods evenly over the course of the hour.

- Using a watch with a second hand, preferably attached to a clipboard, take a 'snapshot' recording every 30 seconds. In practice look at both students at the same 30-second intervals and record the appropriate behaviour category by referring to the 18 DSM-IV ADHD behaviour categories listed at the top of the sheet (page 37). If none is evident, record as 0.

- Record what is happening *at that particular time,* not what has gone on in the meantime.

- Recordings are summarised at a later date in the analysis section. The total numbers of recordings are calculated for each of the three behaviour categories for both students.

 Figure 4.2 Instantaneous time sampling instructions

The ITS schedule devised by the author has modified and extended Lovey's observation sheet. It includes a table listing all 18 ADHD DSM-IV criteria, with a further code of '0' added for 'none of the above behaviours'. There are three recording boxes at the bottom of the sheet consisting of ten-minute time lines with spaces for recordings for the target student and the comparison student at 30-second intervals. An analysis table is included at the bottom of the sheet. The ITS observation schedule is shown in Figure 4.1, with detailed instructions for use in Figure 4.2. These are also available as downloadable materials.

This technique can be used over ten-minute periods to gather quantitative data on frequency, location and sequence of student behaviours. It may be used over three selected periods near to the beginning, middle and end of lessons in order to establish any patterns of behaviour relating to different parts of a lesson. In practice there may be occasional difficulties if the length of the lesson is not known to the observer beforehand. It is therefore helpful if the format of the lesson can be discussed with the teacher in advance, but this is not always possible in practice. This type of observation is useful particularly in lessons which have distinct types of activity at different times, for example the teacher's introduction or demonstration, a class discussion, a written activity, a practical activity of some sort, oral class recapitulation or a question and answer session at the beginning or end of the lesson. Some adjustments and flexibility are often necessary here; for example, the observer might choose to wait until a science experiment is under way before starting the middle observation period.

Fixed interval sampling (FIS)

The fixed interval sampling technique requires the observer to record what has happened during the preceding interval, the length of which can vary from study to study. This enables frequencies to be calculated, simple patterns to be observed and an approximate sequence of events to be noted. Ayers et al. (1996) provide details of a general fixed interval sampling sheet which can be used in the classroom to record behaviours in a series of equal (15-second) time slots using a series of predetermined categories. This sheet was modified by the author for use in the case study research (and referred to as FIS). The FIS observation schedule is shown in Figure 4.3, with detailed instructions for use in Figure 4.4. These are also available as downloadable materials.

During observation periods the observer focuses on the target student and codes each 15-second cell using one of the figures from 0 to 18. In practice, albeit very infrequently, it is sometimes necessary to make informed decisions as to the *predominant* behaviour displayed during each 15-second interval. Categorisation of behaviour can generally be narrowed down into one of the three main DSM-IV behaviour categories. It is possible to use FIS in almost any setting over periods of varying duration, using more than one sheet if necessary. This is particularly useful on occasions when the length of a lesson is not known or is subject to change. This technique can be used on occasions when for some reason there is no opportunity to observe simultaneously the target student and the comparison student. These situations could include observations in a large school hall where the comparison student is not visible or when the target student is working away from the main classroom in a small group with other individuals with SEN.

Fixed Interval Sampling

Recordings of observations of predominant behaviour displayed by target student over 15-second time periods.

Student						Class					No. in Class					Observer					Date	

Activity										Setting												

00	15	30	45	00	15	30	45	00	15	30	45	00	15	30	45	No ADHD	Inatt. (1–9)	Hyp/Imp (10–18)	Behaviour according to DSM-IV criteria
																			Inattention 1. Fails to give close attention to details 2. Difficulty sustaining attention 3. Does not appear to listen
																			4. Difficulty in following through instructions 5. Avoids tasks requiring sustained mental effort
																			6. Difficulty in organising tasks and activities 7. Loses things necessary for tasks and activities
																			8. Easily distracted by extraneous stimuli 9. Forgetful
																			Hyperactivity 10. Fidgets with hands or feet 11. Unauthorised movement in the classroom
																			12. Runs about or climbs excessively in situations where it is inappropriate
																			13. Has difficulty in playing quietly 14. Is often 'on the go' 15. Talks excessively
																			Impulsiveness 16. Blurts out answers 17. Difficulty awaiting turn 18. Interrupts or intrudes upon others (butts in)

Adapted by Linda Wheeler and reproduced with permission from Support for Learning Service, London Borough of Tower Hamlets Children's Services (Ayers, H., Clarke, D. and Ross, A., 1996) *Assessing Individual Needs: A Practical Approach* (2nd edn). London: David Fulton.

Figure 4.3 Fixed interval sampling observation schedule

Fixed Interval Sampling – Instructions

Purpose

- FIS is used to quantify the duration and frequency of predominant behaviours (ADHD or non-ADHD) shown by the target student over the total number of observation periods.

- It involves observation of a target student only.

- It can be used for any length of lesson, if necessary using more than one recording sheet (35 minutes per sheet, i.e. $35 \times 4 = 140$ observations).

Description of instrument

- The recording section on the schedule consists of seven rows each containing five-minute periods which are subdivided into 20 cells. Each cell represents a 15-second period of observation.

- The analysis section consists of three columns for summaries of total recordings for behaviour categories ('No ADHD', 'Inattention' and 'Hyperactive–Impulsive' behaviours).

- DSM-IV criteria for ADHD are listed.

Procedure

- Familiarise yourself with DSM-IV criteria for ADHD.

- Remain as unobtrusive as possible and ideally take no part in the lesson.

- Record at the top of the sheet: the name of the target student; the date and time; the number in the group (e.g. class group, whole school, etc); if there is just a teacher or whether any support is given (e.g. TA offering general support or SSA supporting one particular child); and brief details regarding context and setting.

- Using a watch with a second hand, preferably attached to a clipboard, observe and record in the relevant cell the *predominant* behaviour displayed during fixed interval periods of 15 seconds. Refer to the list of DSM-IV ADHD behaviours numbered 1–18. If none of these are displayed, record as 0.

- In practice if necessary, observe for about 10–12 seconds and use 3–5 seconds to make the recording.

- In some cases a decision has to be made as to the *predominant* behaviour. If it is not possible to ascertain the exact behaviour, aim to identify whether the behaviour comes in one of the main categories, i.e. 'No ADHD', 'Inattention' or 'Hyperactivity/Impulsivity' (these last two are grouped together for analysis purposes).

- Recordings are summarised at a later date in the analysis section. Percentages of the total numbers of recordings are calculated for each of the three behaviour categories.

 Figure 4.4   Fixed interval sampling instructions

Features common to both observation schedules

- Both the FIS and ITS schedules can be used in any early years or school setting. They are practical to use, easy to read and write on and take up one side of a sheet of A4 paper, which easily fits onto a clipboard.

- Using set time periods provides consistency. It is recommended that a watch with a second hand is attached to the clipboard to ensure accuracy of timings (recordings are made every 30 seconds over a period of 10 minutes in ITS and at 15-second intervals for FIS).

- Both schedules include space for recording basic details of context, timings and analysis of recordings. In addition, qualitative field notes should be made where possible to supplement the quantitative data gathered. This is particularly important in ITS where significant developments may have occurred in between the 30-second 'snapshot' recordings.

- There are unavoidably some occasions when during an observation period either the target student is briefly out of sight or the researcher is distracted by a teaching assistant (TA), teacher or student. In these cases the observer can choose to put a dot in the relevant recording boxes and not to include these in the analysis.

- It is suggested that category '10' ('fidgets with hands or feet or squirms in seat') is used for all types of fidgeting or movement not included in other categories. These include leaning back with a chair on two legs, banging feet on the floor, fiddling with hair or clothing and tapping a pencil or ruler on the table.

- It is preferable if the observer is an adult known to both teacher and students and that they remain relatively unobtrusive in the classroom. This may prevent problems with reactivity – where the student's behaviour improves while under observation.

- Begin recording periods using both techniques after the first few minutes of each lesson as these are deemed to be 'settling down periods'.

- In order to add to the validity and reliability of the observational data, it is advisable to undertake as many observations as possible, across contexts and over time.

'On task' or 'No ADHD'?

Research by Daniel and Cooper (1999) used 'on-task' and 'off-task' categories on an observation schedule which employed the antecedents, behaviour and consequences (ABC) approach to observing and analysing classroom behaviour. DuPaul and Stoner describe 'on-task' behaviour as positive student behaviour and define it as 'visual orientation towards assigned task materials for entire interval'. They describe 'off-task' behaviour as negative and define it as 'visual non-attention to one's task or assigned behaviour' (1994: 59–60).

A decision was made to use the term 'No ADHD' for recordings in the case studies when there was no evidence of ADHD behaviours rather than the term 'On task'. This was mainly because early on in the research period there had been several instances when a target student had appeared to be on task but it was discovered either on closer observation or on later inspection of his work that he had in fact been engaged on some other activity, for example drawing a picture instead of carrying out a writing task. Analyses of case study observations used in this chapter and subsequent chapters will use 'No ADHD' rather than 'On task'.

Validity and reliability

Both observation recording schedules were to some extent modifications of existing instruments. It was therefore necessary for the author to establish the validity and reliability of the instantaneous time sampling (ITS) and fixed interval sampling (FIS) schedules. The internal validity and coherence of the content of the items used in both schedules is based on the use of the 18 ADHD characteristics described in DSM-IV, the most recent edition of the diagnostic criteria for ADHD (APA, 2000). A regular updating process for DSM criteria takes into account such factors as any new diagnoses, results of field trials and tests of validity. Every possible effort has been made to establish face validity and content validity in these quantitative observation methods.

As a single observer carried out the case study observations, it was necessary for inter-rater reliability of the schedules to be established. This involved the recording of observations of videotaped extracts of children's classroom behaviour by three observers on different occasions, resulting in an inter-rater reliability figure of 97 per cent. The reliability of the research findings was enhanced by the longitudinal element of the case studies. Consistency of observation data was achieved by the repeated use of systematic observation schedules on different days and times and in different curricular settings over a two-year period (Wheeler, 2007).

Analysis of observation data

As mentioned previously, information from both ITS and FIS observations may be used to calculate the proportion of time spent by the target student in displaying ADHD behaviour, and also the time spent not displaying ADHD behaviour. Analysis of ITS findings also offers opportunities for comparison with the behaviour of a non-ADHD student and identification of variability in the target student's performance in different parts of lessons. In drawing any conclusions regarding the observational data, it is important to refer to any background notes which may have been made on the context in which the observations took place. Certain situations might influence the behaviour of the target student and/or the comparison student during particular observation periods. These might include the following:

• changes to routine, including a supply teacher taking the lesson;

• the time of the day, the day of the week, the beginning or end of a school term;

• the weather;

• a target student having forgotten to take his medication.

When analysing the data on both ITS and FIS sheets, three behaviour columns headed 'No ADHD', 'Inattention' and 'Hyperactive/Impulsive' are used. This is mainly due to the fact that diagnosis of ADHD using DSM-IV diagnostic criteria

Instantaneous Time Sampling

Behaviour according to DSM-IV criteria		
Inattention	**Hyperactivity**	**Impulsiveness**
1. Fails to give close attention to details 2. Difficulty sustaining attention 3. Does not appear to listen 4. Difficulty in following through instructions 5. Avoids tasks requiring sustained mental effort 6. Difficulty in organising tasks and activities 7. Loses things necessary for tasks and activities 8. Easily distracted by extraneous stimuli 9. Forgetful	10. Fidgets with hands or feet or squirms in seat 11. Unauthorised movement in the classroom 12. Runs about or climbs excessively in situations where it is inappropriate 13. Has difficulty in playing quietly 14. Is often 'on the go' 15. Talks excessively	16. Blurts out answers 17. Difficulty awaiting turn 18. Interrupts or intrudes upon others (butts in) 0. None of the above behaviours

Date	Time	Context: *Literacy lesson – class group, teacher, SSA*
Wed 30 April	*11:18*	*On carpet, re-cap report-writing, based on Big Book*
	11:38	*Writing individual reports, sitting at tables*
	11:54	*On carpet. Some read out work*

Recordings of observations of target student and comparison behaviours taken at 30-second intervals for a 10-minute period

T	2	0	0	2	2	8	2	10	2	2	0	2	0	10	0	0	2	2	2	2
	1	2	3	4	5	6	7	8	9	10	11	12	13	14	15	16	17	18	19	20
C	0	0	0	2	2	0	0	0	10	10	0	0	0	0	0	0	2	2	2	0

T	0	0	0	0	0	0	0	0	11	0	0	0	0	0	0	0	0	8	8	0
	1	2	3	4	5	6	7	8	9	10	11	12	13	14	15	16	17	18	19	20
C	0	0	0	0	0	0	0	0	0	0	2	0	0	0	0	0	0	2	0	2

T	0	0	10	10	0	0	2	0	0	0	8	2	2	10	0	0	18	2	0	18
	1	2	3	4	5	6	7	8	9	10	11	12	13	14	15	16	17	18	19	20
C	0	0	2	2	0	0	0	0	0	0	0	0	0	2	0	0	0	0	0	2

Analysis

Time	Context	Target: *David*			Comparison: *John*		
		No ADHD	Inattention	Hyp/Imp	No ADHD	Inattention	Hyp/Imp
11:18	*Carpet, recap*	6	12	2	13	5	2
11:38	*Writing report*	17	2	1	17	3	0
11:54	*Carpet*	9	6	5	16	4	0
Totals		32/60	20/60	8/60	46/60	12/60	2/60
Percentages		54%	33%	13%	77%	20%	3%

Figure 4.5 Example of ITS analysis

demands six or more symptoms of inattention and/or six or more symptoms of hyperactivity–impulsivity (APA, 2000). However, as the observation recordings are based on all 18 DSM-IV criteria (plus 0 for 'No ADHD'), more detailed data would be available if more in-depth analyses were required.

Analysis of instantaneous time sampling (ITS)

As shown in Figure 4.5, the numbers of recordings made for each behaviour category are summarised in the analysis section at the bottom of the observation sheet. For both target and comparison students in each 10-minute period:

- all recordings for 0 are included in the 'No ADHD' column;

- recordings of categories 1–9 are totalled and included in the 'Inattention' column;

- recordings of categories 10–18 are totalled and included in the 'Hyperactive–Impulsive' (Hyp–Imp) column.

It is possible to see at a glance any differences between the 'scores' out of 20 for 'No ADHD' and ADHD behaviours recorded for the two students. If further analysis is required, the scores out of 20 may be converted into percentages. During the three observation periods undertaken during the literacy lesson shown in Figure 4.5 it can be seen that the target student displayed 28/60 ADHD behaviours compared to the non-ADHD student's 14/20. The analysis shows that the target student displayed fewer ADHD behaviours during the middle recording session when engaged in a desk-based writing task (in fact his score of 17/20 for 'No ADHD' behaviour matched the comparison's score). On this occasion the teacher provided David with the opportunity to concentrate on his work by moving him to a table to work on his own where he would not be distracted by other students. It was clear that David found more difficulty in concentrating and keeping still when sitting on the carpet at the beginning and end of the lesson when he had nothing on which to focus and when there were more distractions. Interestingly, John, the comparison student, also displayed more ADHD behaviours during the carpet sessions than when engaged on the writing task.

Analysis of fixed interval sampling (FIS)

Figure 4.6 shows how straightforward it is to calculate the proportions or percentages of each behaviour category displayed by the target student during the observation period. As with ITS (above):

- all recordings for 0 are included in the 'No ADHD' column;

- recordings of categories 1–9 are totalled and included in the 'Inattention' column;

- recordings of categories 10–18 are totalled and included in the 'Hyperactive–Impulsive' (Hyp–Imp) column.

An examination of the FIS analysis of the group literacy lesson shown in Figure 4.6 reveals that Carl displayed 'No ADHD' behaviours for 55 per cent of the 20-minute recording period. Of the 45 per cent ADHD behaviours recorded, 28 per cent were for

Example of Fixed Interval Sampling

Recordings of observations of predominant behaviour displayed by target student over 15-second time periods.

Student	Class	Age	No. in Group	Date	Observer
Carl		9–10 years	4	Wed 4th Dec	LW

Activity: Literacy lesson – observation began at 11.50 am

Setting: T, TA in withdrawal area – guided reading

00	15	30	45	00	15	30	45	00	15	30	45	00	15	30	45	No ADHD	Inatt. (1–9)	Hy/Imp (10–18)
10	2	2	0	0	0	0	8	0	0	16	0					15	3	2
0	0	2	8	0	0	0	0	0	8	10	8					10	6	4
0	10	0	0	8	2	2	0	0	10	0	0					11	6	3
0	10	10	0	0	2	2	0	10	2	2	2					8	7	5
																44/80	22/80	14/80
																55%	28%	17%

Behaviour according to DSM-IV criteria

Inattention
1. Fails to give close attention to details
2. Difficulty sustaining attention
3. Does not appear to listen
4. Difficulty in following through instructions
5. Avoids tasks requiring sustained mental effort
6. Difficulty in organising tasks and activities
7. Loses things necessary for tasks and activities
8. Easily distracted by extraneous stimuli
9. Forgetful

Hyperactivity
10. Fidgets with hands or feet
11. Unauthorised movement in the classroom
12. Runs about or climbs excessively in situations where it is inappropriate
13. Has difficulty in playing quietly
14. Is often 'on the go'
15. Talks excessively

Impulsiveness
16. Blurts out answers
17. Difficulty awaiting turn
18. Interrupts or intrudes upon others (butts in)

Adapted by Linda Wheeler and reproduced with permission from Support for Learning Service, London Borough of Tower Hamlets Children's Services (Ayers, H., Clarke, D. and Ross, A., 1996) *Assessing Individual Needs: A Practical Approach* (2nd edn). London: David Fulton.

Figure 4.6 Exampe of FIS analysis

'inattention' and 17 per cent were for 'hyperactive–impulsive' behaviours. He appeared to pay more attention during the first five-minute period (when he displayed 15/20 'No ADHD' behaviour) than in subsequent periods. During the last five minutes he displayed 7/20 'inattention' and 5/20 'hyperactive–impulsive' behaviours. Throughout the lesson, Carl had received plenty of support and encouragement from the SENCO and TA but he was finding it increasingly difficult to concentrate towards lunchtime.

Practical applications of systematic observation techniques

Observational data gathered using systematic techniques in educational settings can be useful in numerous ways to educational, healthcare and other professionals. The following three practical applications were identified during the case study research.

To facilitate the gathering of practice-based evidence in assessment processes

The need for classroom observation of individual students in multi-professional working has been highlighted in the previous chapter. Some questionnaires and rating scales employed by clinicians to gather information from schools (and parents) often tend to use Likert-type scales. These involve the respondent indicating frequency of behaviours by, for example, circling items: 0 (*never or rarely*) to 3 (*very often*). Anecdotal evidence may also be supplied by teachers and parents, but this may be subject to bias or inaccuracy. More use of systematic observation techniques providing detailed quantitative evidence on behaviour could be used to supplement other data during the identification and assessment of ADHD.

Schools are required to gather evidence of an individual's learning difficulties or challenging behaviour in all assessment processes, whether they are seeking provision or support under the SEN Code of Practice procedures or they are intending to put a student forward for possible diagnosis of a disorder such as ADHD. When an Individual Education Plan (IEP) has been drawn up, quantitative evidence can be used to supplement anecdotal or qualitative details provided by teaching staff.

 Case study

Carl's Individual Education Plan

During the first year of the case study one of the targets on Carl's IEP was: 'To maintain 70 per cent "on task" behaviour during literacy lessons'.

Over the course of the autumn term, using fixed interval sampling (FIS), it was possible for the researcher to calculate that, over the eight literacy lessons when observations took place, Carl achieved an average of 69 per cent 'No ADHD' behaviour, 17 per cent 'Inattention' behaviour and 14 per cent 'Hyperactive–Impulsive' behaviour. These findings were discussed with the SENCO and class teacher.

Although these findings could not be used in isolation, when added to other informal observations made by teaching staff during the term it was possible to see that Carl had more or less achieved one of his IEP targets. Some of the other case study findings in which Carl displayed a higher proportion of ADHD behaviours were included by the SENCO in applications for statutory assessment which led to a Statement of SEN being issued the following year.

To help in monitoring the effects of medication or other interventions

Hughes and Cooper (2007) stress the importance of schools identifying tools with which to monitor behaviour change in students with ADHD. By examining observational data on the variability of ADHD behaviours *over time* as well as *across settings* the following extracts from two case studies demonstrate that FIS in particular can be used for this purpose. In each case it was possible to use the systematic observation findings to supplement the anecdotal evidence from school staff regarding changes in behaviour.

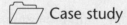 Case study

Adam – before and after medication

Adam had been diagnosed with ADHD and prescribed Ritalin at the beginning of the second year of the case study. The comparisons made of variability over time are therefore not only between his recorded behaviours in the first and second year of the case study, but also between those before and after starting to take medication.

Figure 4.7 shows that, across all FIS observations, the proportion of lessons Adam spent displaying 'Hyperactive–Impulsive' (Hyp–Imp) behaviours decreased significantly from 10 per cent in the first year of the case study to 4 per cent in

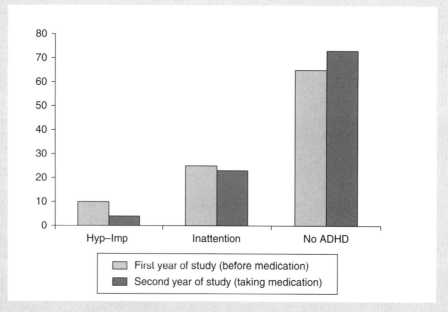

Figure 4.7   FIS recordings over time (all settings) – Adam

the second year. Recordings for 'Inattention' fell from 25 to 23 per cent and 'No ADHD' behaviours increased from 65 per cent in the first year to 73 per cent the following year.

 Case study

Edward – effects of increase in medication

Edward, aged 7 years at the beginning of the case study, had been taking Ritalin since the age of 5 years and had shown gradual improvement in his behaviour. Three years later teaching staff reported a noticeable deterioration in his behaviour which posed management problems for the school. An increase in Edward's medication dose halfway through the spring term brought about a vast improvement in his concentration and behaviour. As this was the term in which the second year of the case study was undertaken it was possible for the researcher to observe first-hand the changes in Edward's behaviour.

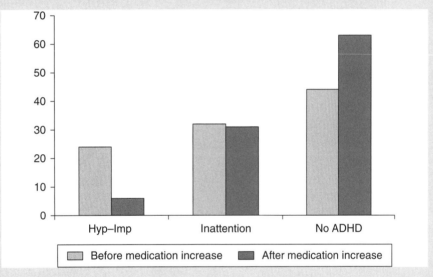

Figure 4.8 FIS recordings before and after increase in medication – Edward

Analysis of the FIS observations (shown in Figure 4.8) found that during the second year of the case study Edward's overall recorded figure for 'Hyperactive–Impulsive' behaviours in observed lessons during the period prior to the increased medication was 24 per cent, decreasing dramatically to 6 per cent after the increase. 'Inattentive' behaviours reduced from 32 to 31 per cent and consequently there was an increase in 'No ADHD' behaviours from 44 to 63 per cent.

To identify contextual and curricular settings and approaches which may help teachers to enhance on-task behaviour

Systematic observations undertaken in the case studies have produced a wide range of context-unique data on the situational and temporal variability of ADHD behaviour in mainstream schools, allowing identification to be made of settings, interventions and approaches aimed at increasing on-task behaviour in students displaying characteristics associated with ADHD (Wheeler, 2007). As previously mentioned, each individual who displays ADHD characteristics is unique. Interventions which help one student may not be of benefit to another student. Approaches adopted in one setting might not produce the same effects on subsequent occasions or in different settings. The following examples demonstrate different ways in which observational data can be analysed. Fergal's case study extract focuses on variability in behaviour recorded in lessons in one curriculum area.

 Case study

Fergal – variability in behaviour with different teachers

During the second year of the case study it was clear that Fergal's behaviour fluctuated across lessons according to teachers. Figure 4.9 clearly demonstrates the marked variability in his behaviour observed in numeracy lessons. When taught in the maths set taken by his registration class teacher, he displayed 5 per cent 'Hyperactive–Impulsive', 13 per cent 'Inattentive' and 82 per cent 'No ADHD' behaviours. When a supply teacher took the lesson, Fergal's figures were 30 per cent 'Hyperactive–Impulsive', 25 per cent 'Inattentive' and 45 per cent 'No ADHD' behaviours.

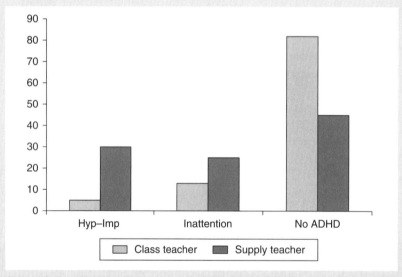

Figure 4.9   FIS recordings for numeracy lesson with different teachers – Fergal

Fergal's registration class teacher had previous experience in working with students with SEN and had built up a good relationship with him. He found changes to routine very difficult to cope with.

It may not be possible for the school to act on these findings due to financial and organisational constraints and there are often unavoidable changes to routine, but by identifying and quantifying the differences in Fergal's behaviour over time there may be the possibility of obtaining extra classroom support for him, for example each time a supply teacher takes a lesson.

The observation analyses in the extract from Carl's case study shown below highlight variability in an individual student's behaviour in different curriculum areas and on different occasions. This information may be useful in future planning for the delivery and organisation of the curriculum.

 Case study

Carl – variability in behaviour across settings

Date, time, duration of recording	Context	No ADHD	ADHD behaviours	
			Inattention	Hyp–Imp
(i) Wed 23 Oct 11:00 – 60 minutes	**Music** – half class, n = 14, in corner of hall with music teacher. Play instruments, practise tune.	81%	10%	9%
(ii) Fri 15 Nov 10:20 – 28 minutes	**Whole-school assembly**, n = approx. 420 in school hall, with head teacher and teachers.	28%	34%	38%

Figure 4.10   Extracts from fixed interval sampling observation analysis – Carl

(i) For the weekly music lesson the class was split into two, with Carl's half going into the school hall to work with the visiting music teacher while the other half stayed in the classroom for other activities with the class teacher. After the music teacher's introduction when Carl was fidgeting, he seemed to enjoy the lesson. He was especially pleased when he was chosen to play a xylophone. Placed by the teacher in between two girls, he concentrated, tried hard to play the right notes and performed well. The small numbers of his 'inattentive' and 'hyperactive' behaviours were usually when the teacher was talking to other students individually and he was keen to start playing again.

(ii) In contrast to the above extract, it can be seen that Carl found it difficult to concentrate in a school assembly. He often had difficulty coping in this type of situation, with so many distractions in the school hall filled with children. The teacher tried to sit him next to a good role model, but this did not always help. The field notes show that this particular day was 'Children in Need' day and there was an air of excitement throughout the school. Various fundraising activities were being carried out and the timing of the assembly had been rearranged by the head teacher. Usually first thing in the morning following registration, it now followed the literacy lesson, just before playtime. Carl had

(Continued)

(Continued)

difficulty coping with so many changes to routine (Cooper and Bilton, 2002). This is an example of one of the situations where it is difficult for school staff to offer sufficient support for the individual with ADHD. One suggestion is for the teacher to try to 'create time for the child to move around and chatter before the assembly, followed by a calming down period' (O'Regan, 2002: 20).

Date, time at which 10-minute recording period began, part of lesson	Lesson	Recordings out of 20					
		Target student Carl			Comparison student Ian		
		0	ADHD behaviours		0	ADHD behaviours	
			Inatt	H/I		Inatt	H/I
(i) Thur 20 Nov 11:30 – Start	**Science** – Class, then groups Write up yesterday's experiment	5	12	3	13	6	1
11:50 – Middle	Writing, T introduces experiment	16	4	0	18	2	0
12:02 – End	Experiments – separating solids.	20	0	0	20	0	0
(ii) Tues 15 Oct 14:03 – Start	**Science** – Class Devise tables – 'Changes'	6	5	9	16	3	1
14:27 – Middle	Class discussion – share ideas	6	7	7	15	3	2
14:40 – End	Draw cross-section of fruit.	5	9	6	14	4	2

Figure 4.11 Extracts from instantaneous time sampling observation analysis – Carl

(i) Science was one of Carl's favourite lessons. In this lesson the class worked in groups of four and a TA was in the classroom offering support to Carl and another boy. The start of the lesson included a brief recap and writing up of the experiment undertaken the previous day. Carl needed a lot of support to maintain his attention. In the middle of the lesson when the teacher (T) was preparing the class for the experiments, Carl was able to concentrate and sustain attention almost as often as Ian. The TA occasionally asked Carl a direct question to bring him back on task. She was also able to write down Carl's ideas to save time. She discussed his ideas with him and encouraged him to share them with the rest of the group. As the lesson progressed the TA gradually withdrew her support as Carl became totally focused on the experimental activity during which he paid as much attention as Ian.

(ii) In addition to science lessons, Carl also enjoyed drawing, was usually happy to contribute to class discussions and often had good ideas to put forward. At the beginning of this science lesson, following the teacher's introduction, the children were required to show in tabular form 'How we change as we grow up'. Carl was one of the students allowed to use pictures rather than writing. Later in the lesson there was a class discussion when the children were sharing ideas. During both of these parts of the lesson Carl was noticeably more hyperactive and inattentive than Ian. Towards the end of the lesson the task was to draw a cross-section of one of several pieces of fruit. Carl again found great difficulty in paying attention and remaining still and Ian did not pay as much attention as he usually did. Interestingly, the field notes record that on this particular day it rained nearly all day. This meant that there was no opportunity for the children to get any physical exercise in the playground. Carl's 'No ADHD' behaviour was poor for all lessons that day. Even in a science lesson that he would normally have enjoyed he was unable to pay attention. Another contributory factor to the differences in Carl's behaviour may have been the lack of any support from a teaching assistant during this lesson.

This chapter has provided a comprehensive introduction to two systematic observation techniques which can be used in all educational settings, including early years, primary and secondary schools. After a brief familiarisation period, any adult with experience of working in an educational setting should soon become proficient in the use of both FIS and ITS techniques. The schedules have been designed by the author specifically for use in school settings when identifying and monitoring students who display behaviour associated with ADHD. Their extensive use over a two-year period in a wide variety of school settings has enabled the identification of any practical problems which are likely to occur. Blank analysis tables are provided in Appendices E and F (also available as downloadable materials). Chapter 5 will focus on more in-depth analyses of observational data on variability in ADHD behaviour across settings, over time and between cases to identify contextual and curricular approaches for use in enhancing on-task behaviour.

 Points to remember

- Systematic classroom observation is important in the management of students who display ADHD behaviours.
- Each student is unique.
- Data from systematic observation has practical applications in schools.
- Observations should be carried out across settings and over time.
- It is important to supplement quantitative observation data with qualitative background details.

 Questions for reflection and discussion

1. Does your school have an effective system for recording students' behaviour?
2. Would you feel confident in carrying out systematic observation in school settings?

 Remember: The instantaneous time sampling (ITS) and fixed interval sampling (FIS) observation schedules and instructions for use (Figures 4.1, 4.2, 4.3 and 4.4) and blank analysis tables (Appendices E and F) are also available from www.sagepub.co.uk/wheeler

5

Effective teaching for students with ADHD

By examining variability in ADHD behaviour across settings, over time and between cases, this chapter focuses on a range of effective teaching and management approaches for use with students displaying characteristics associated with ADHD. Drawing on findings from case study research and where appropriate taking into account theories concerning the nature of ADHD, the discussion focuses on:

- the positive aspects of ADHD characteristics;
- the delivery and organisation of the curriculum;
- teaching and learning styles;
- grouping and support in the classroom; and
- school training needs.

In providing effective teaching for students with ADHD, the positive aspects of ADHD characteristics should be taken into account and built into the delivery and organisation of lessons. As Cooper suggests, use should be made of 'pedagogical strategies designed to exploit, rather than inhibit, some of the characteristics associated with ADHD' (2005: 130). Positive attributes may include:

- the ability to focus deeply on selected topics;

- divergent thinking;

- being highly imaginative, innovative and inquisitive;

- sensitivity;

- creativity;

- tremendous energy;

- a willingness to take risks;

- enthusiasm;

- curiosity;

- a sense of humour.

This chapter identifies effective contextual and curricular approaches by closely examining findings from the case studies and where appropriate taking into account theories concerning the nature of ADHD. As mentioned in Chapter 4, the term 'No ADHD' behaviours was used rather than 'on task' throughout the case studies. By analysing the data from each individual case study as well as across cases it was possible to ascertain 'average' figures for the proportion of 'ADHD' and 'No ADHD' behaviours displayed in observed lessons over the research period using both types of systematic observation. The average fixed interval sampling (FIS) 'No ADHD' percentage across the six target students was 66 per cent and the average instantaneous time sampling (ITS) 'No ADHD' percentage was 55 per cent (11/20), with a figure for the comparison students of 86 per cent (17/20). Further analysis has identified contexts in which fewer than average 'ADHD' behaviours (or more 'No ADHD' behaviours) were displayed (Wheeler, 2007). The following three sections, based on findings from the six case studies, offer suggestions for settings and approaches which may help teachers to enhance on-task behaviour in students with ADHD.

Delivery and organisation of the curriculum

Use of computers and videos

Research has shown that the inhibitory performance of individuals with ADHD might be context dependent (Barkley, 2006) and that one of the areas in which they perform as well as typically developing students is in the use of computers (Shaw et al., 2005). This could explain the case study findings in which observation recordings of 'No ADHD' behaviours for all six target students in information and communication technology (ICT) lessons were higher than average and the students seemed able to sustain attention. Individuals with ADHD were also able to sustain attention when watching a video or television programme in school.

 Case studies

Sanjay – use of computer and video

Date, time, duration	Context	No ADHD	ADHD behaviours	
			Inattention	Hyperactivity/ Impulsivity
(i) Thur 11 Dec 10:36 – 70 minutes	**ICT** – n = 20 students from across year group, in ICT suite. Each child customises and prints off a photo of themselves for a calendar.	81%	8%	11%
(ii) Thur 14 Nov 13:17 – 91 minutes	**History** – n = 90 (year group), then 34 (class). Year group watch video; class discuss then design poster; ICT.	78%	9%	13%

Figure 5.1 Sanjay: use of computers and video – extracts from fixed interval sampling observations

(Continued)

(Continued)

(i) Sanjay enjoyed working on the computer. During this lesson he was much more focused and able to concentrate. Most children sat with partners to work on the computers but Sanjay chose to work on his own. The teacher offered him plenty of support throughout the lesson and on one or two occasions Sanjay was happy to call over to other children who offered him peer support. Most of his hyperactive–impulsive behaviours were towards the end of the lesson when Sanjay was waiting for the teacher's attention.

(ii) Sanjay was able to pay attention in only some of the activities during this history lesson. It began with the students from three classes from the same year group watching a video of a history programme about the Second World War in Sanjay's classroom. Even though there were opportunities for Sanjay to become distracted, with approximately 90 students sitting on the classroom floor, he was totally focused on the television throughout the 15-minute programme. After the other classes had left, Sanjay's class stayed on the carpet for a teacher-led discussion about the programme and also about designing and making individual 'Dig for Victory' posters. During this session Sanjay became more fidgety and distracted and at the end it was clear that he had not understood the teacher's instructions as he had copied the teacher's example from the board instead of designing his own poster. For the final 15 minutes of the lesson Sanjay was allowed to use a class computer and he sustained attention for approximately 15 minutes.

Date, time at which 10-minute recording period began, part of lesson	Lesson	Recordings out of 20					
		Target student			Comparison student		
		0	ADHD behaviours		0	ADHD behaviours	
			Inatt	H/I		Inatt	H/I
(i) David/John Wed 5 Feb 14:11 – Start	**ICT** – Class – 'Colour Magic': On carpet, T demonstrates	18	1	1	19	1	0
14:30 – Middle	Working in pairs on computers	17	2	1	18	2	0
14:46 – End	On computers, then end on carpet.	12	1	7	16	3	1
(ii) Carl/Ian Mon 15 Sep 13:36 – Start	**History** – 2 x classes: Watch video – 'The Victorians'	16	1	3	20	0	0
13:57 – Middle	Class brainstorming session	3	8	9	11	6	3
14:28 – End	Writing, worksheets.	5	12	3	13	7	0

Figure 5.2 Use of computer and video – extracts from instantaneous time sampling observations

David – use of computer

(i) The art lesson taken in the ICT suite focused on the use of a programme called 'Colour Magic'. Following the teacher's introduction David coincidentally chose John, the comparison student, to be his partner and they worked cooperatively together, with John offering peer support which included 'saving' their work at the end. David's behaviour compared favourably with that of John at the start and in the middle of the lesson. Towards the end of the lesson David occasionally sought reassurance and praise from the teacher or teaching assistant, sometimes following one of them around the room. He became more fidgety during the final carpet session, displaying more hyperactive–impulsive behaviours.

Carl – use of video

(ii) The first observation period in this history lesson was carried out when the two classes from the same year group joined up to watch a video in the neighbouring classroom. It can be seen that having something interesting on which to focus enabled Carl to pay attention almost as much as did Ian. This was despite the fact that the room was quite crowded and some children were sitting on the floor. For the middle and end of the lesson the children had returned to their own classrooms for follow-up activities involving an oral brainstorming session followed by written work. Neither Carl nor Ian concentrated as well as when they were watching the video.

Computers offer a multi-sensory experience and instant response, are non-judgemental and non-threatening and provide constant feedback and reinforcement. The individual can control the pace and retry problems. It is important that software is carefully chosen and that teachers guard against frustrations arising from any technical problems (O'Regan, 2002). Obviously computers cannot take the place of teachers, but computer-assisted instruction can use software to supplement teacher instruction and to provide additional exposure to academic material. More use of computer-based tasks in the classroom for students with ADHD might offer opportunities for improvements in their academic performance, appropriate on-task performance and behaviour. Where appropriate the inclusion of short videos in lessons can also help students to sustain attention.

Novel approaches

ADHD behaviour may be minimal or absent when the individual is in a novel setting or is engaged in an activity which they find especially interesting. The following extracts demonstrate that higher than average percentages for 'No ADHD' behaviour were often recorded in case studies when students were involved in novel situations.

Case studies

Novel approaches

Date, time at which 10-minute recording period began, part of lesson	Lesson	Recordings out of 20					
		Target student			Comparison student		
		0	ADHD behaviours		0	ADHD behaviours	
			Inatt	H/I		Inatt	H/I
(i) Edward/Kai Thur 6 Feb	**Numeracy** – 'Division':						
11:30 – Start	Class on carpet, practical activity	19	1	0	20	0	0
11:40 – Middle	As above, then in groups	6	12	2	17	2	1
11:50 – End	Practical 'division' activity	6	7	7	16	4	0
(ii) Fergal/Neil Tues 29 Jun	**Firemen visit** – Home Safety:						
10:08 – Start	Talk on smoke alarms, fireman 1	20	0	0	20	0	0
10:18 – Middle	As above	18	2	0	18	2	0
10:29 – Middle	House fire escape plan, fireman 2	17	2	1	19	1	0
10:40 – End	As above	14	5	1	17	3	0
(iii) Adam/Georgio Wed 12 Nov							
14:25 – Start	**History** – 'Anglo-Saxons': Teacher recap in classroom	8	8	4	17	3	0
14:41 – Middle	'Archaeology dig' outside	16	4	0	18	2	0
15:00 – End	Finish dig, then in classroom	8	9	3	14	5	1

Figure 5.3   Novel approaches – extracts from instantaneous time sampling observations

Edward – numeracy lesson

(i) Edward was generally unable to pay attention in any numeracy lessons, but there is one notable exception. In this lesson the teacher began by using chocolate 'Smarties' sweets in a practical demonstration of division sums. A group at a time stood up and were handed sweets to use in several practical activities, at the end of which the students were allowed to eat their 'Smarties'. The whole class concentrated in this part of the lesson, and Edward almost managed to match Kai in paying attention. In the middle and at the end of the lesson when the groups worked at tables on worksheets and other practical activities using multi-link cubes, Edward found it very difficult to focus, even with TA support. He was noticeably much more inattentive and hyperactive than Kai.

Fergal – visit from firemen

(ii) Fergal more or less matched Neil's 'No ADHD' behaviour throughout most of a talk given to the class by two local firemen on this visit to the school. It was only towards the end of the session that Fergal began to lose his concentration. The novelty of the situation and TA support probably helped ensure he maintained his attention early on, together with the promise that the class would later be allowed to look round the fire appliance outside.

Adam – history lesson

(iii) This history lesson began in the classroom where the teacher recapped previous work on Anglo-Saxon archaeology and artefacts. Adam had difficulty sustaining attention, fidgeted and blurted out answers, unlike Georgio who was able to pay attention for most of the time. The teacher then divided the class into groups of four, taking care to group Adam with three good role models, for the next part of the lesson. This 'archaeological dig' took place outside in the school grounds. The teacher had previously buried pieces of broken pottery and the children had to dig them up. Adam worked cooperatively with his group, his behaviour comparing favourably with Georgio's. The lesson ended back in the classroom. When the teacher was explaining what they would do the following day with the pieces of pottery Adam again fidgeted and found it difficult to concentrate.

Innovative or 'out of the ordinary' ideas for delivering and organising the curriculum can often grab the attention of the student who would normally have difficulty in concentrating or focusing in a lesson. It is also important to get to know what particular interests individual students may have and to take these into account when planning how to deliver lessons.

Physical exercise in school

On many occasions during the case study research, higher levels of ADHD behaviours were recorded during less structured lessons which may not have provided sufficient stimulation for target students. Individuals with ADHD were observed to move around the classroom on some pretext more often than did their non-ADHD peers. They would go over to the bin to sharpen pencils (often unnecessarily) or ask permission to go to the toilet or to get a drink. This behaviour, although often more acceptable in an early years or primary setting than a high school setting, can disrupt the flow of lessons. Cooper (2005) suggests that increases in on-task behaviour and reductions in disruptive behaviour can be achieved if periods of 'seat-work' involving cognitive tasks are punctuated by frequent periods of structured physical activity. This could be particularly useful, for example, on 'wet play' days when children miss out on opportunities to move about in the playground (see for example the second science extract in Carl's case study in the previous chapter).

Situations where higher numbers of ADHD behaviours are displayed

In addition to previously mentioned situations such as 'wet play' days and changes to routine including supply teachers taking lessons, there are inevitably some school settings where, however much support is provided, the student with ADHD is unable to remain on task. In school-hall activities such as assembly or hymn practice and lessons that are often less structured than core subjects children with ADHD can find it difficult to concentrate. In lessons such as music and PE where students showed some variability in behaviour, the higher levels of ADHD behaviours were displayed during less structured activities which may not have provided sufficient stimulation for target students. Edward, Fergal and Adam all displayed such hyperactive behaviour in an unstructured PE lesson in the school hall that each one was sent out of a lesson as they were considered a danger to themselves and to the other students.

Teaching and learning styles

There is often a focus on reflective and abstract teaching and learning in schools rather than the concrete and active learning styles favoured by individuals with ADHD (Cooper, 2005). Creative activities such as art, Design and Technology (DT) and practical science lessons in which all six target students displayed lower levels of ADHD behaviours rely on active experimentation using kinaesthetic (or non-traditional) teaching and learning approaches. The case study findings agree with Daniel and Cooper (1999) who reported that students displayed lower levels of dysfunctional behaviour in lessons involving sensory and kinaesthetic skills. In addition, as Carl's DT lesson in Figure 5.4 demonstrates (see case study below), 'creative students can often be a valuable resource to the classroom teacher in their ability to offer divergent ways of looking at things or novel approaches to problems' (Cooper and Bilton, 2002: 69). It is important that students with ADHD are not taken out of art and DT lessons for extra tuition in core subjects as this could undermine the positive reinforcement offered by creative activities (O'Regan, 2002).

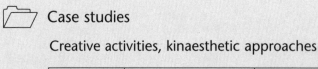 Case studies

Creative activities, kinaesthetic approaches

Date, time, duration	Context	No ADHD	ADHD behaviours	
			Inattention	Hyperactivity/ Impulsivity
(i) Carl Thur 4 Dec 13:54 – 35 minutes	**DT** – half class, n = 12, outside main classroom, with teacher. Modifying model of chassis, adding motor.	88%	9%	3%
(ii) Edward Mon 9 Feb 14:02 – 19 minutes	**Art** – Class group, painting on black paper, picture made up of different coloured 'dots' (pointillism).	84%	16%	0

Figure 5.4   Creative activities – extracts from fixed interval sampling observations

Carl – DT

(i) Carl was able to pay attention and concentrate during most of this DT lesson. He worked in a group of 12 children outside the main classroom area with the (male) teacher, while a TA oversaw the rest of the class in the classroom. The teacher was able to offer plenty of support and encouragement to Carl in modifying a model of a chassis which he had started to make the previous week. He carefully supervised Carl, who demonstrated creativity in using three wheels on his chassis, unlike the majority of others who used four wheels. Carl had made a useful suggestion as to the best place to fix a motor to a model and the teacher asked him to explain this to the rest of the group. The following week, the teacher suggested that Carl should be awarded a merit badge from the head teacher for his work in DT. By drawing attention to Carl's good work and ideas the teacher helped to boost Carl's self-esteem and enabled his peers to see that Carl could make a positive contribution to classroom activities (Cooper and Bilton, 2002).

Edward – art

(ii) Edward enjoyed creative activities and was often able to sustain attention during art lessons. In this lesson the added novelty of using the 'wrong' end of the paint brush with which to paint a picture made up of dots particularly seemed to appeal to him. He was able to focus on the task for the majority of the lesson. His inattentive behaviours were generally when he was occasionally distracted by his classmates, some of whom

Date, time at which 10-minute recording period began, part of lesson	Lesson	Recordings out of 20					
		Target student			Comparison student		
		0	ADHD behaviours		0	ADHD behaviours	
			Inatt	H/I		Inatt	H/I
(i) Carl/Ian Mon 25 Nov	**Art** – group, n = 5, in art area:						
14:00 – Start	Apply hot wax to Batik	18	1	1	19	1	0
14:24 – Middle	Draw design on piece of material	17	3	0	16	4	0
14:44 – End	Reapply hot wax	18	2	0	19	1	0
(ii) David/John Mon 12 May	**DT** – design picnic container:						
13:39 – Start	On carpet for T's introduction	15	4	1	15	5	0
13:53 – Middle}	{Working at tables on {making	16	3	1	17	3	0
14:05 – Middle}	prototype model	20	0	0	19	1	0
14:28 – End	Sit in circle on carpet, show work	10	4	6	10	6	4

Figure 5.5 Creative activities – extracts from instantaneous time sampling observations

(Continued)

(Continued)

were engaged in reading to the teacher or drawing activities following completion of the main task.

Carl – art

(i) Carl enjoyed creative activities and was pleased to be one of the first chosen by the class teacher to work with a TA and a parent helper in the art area during the art lesson on Batik. After giving the class a talk on the safety aspects of using hot wax, the teacher had trusted Carl to be sensible and safety conscious. She also gave him the responsibility of going to another classroom to ask for some paint overalls. This interesting and unusual activity involving fabric printing particularly held his attention throughout the lesson. His behaviour compared favourably with that of Ian, his non-ADHD classmate.

David – DT

(ii) Throughout most of this DT lesson when four observation periods were undertaken, David had the support of a teaching assistant. She offered plenty of encouragement and praise as he made a prototype paper picnic basket. David paid attention from the start, matching John's 'No ADHD' behaviour. While working on his model he continued to sustain his attention for much of the time. Both students were more inattentive and hyperactive during the final period when the class sat in a circle on the carpet to show their models.

Grouping and support

There is a need for flexibility in student grouping in classroom settings. Findings from observations in the case studies indicate that ability grouping in curricular areas such as literacy may increase attainment. All six target students were included in small ability groups for some or all literacy lessons. In the cases of Carl and Adam these groups were regularly taken by teaching assistants, following planning with SENCOs, while the more able groups were taught by teachers. A possible drawback to rigid arrangements for ability groups across the curriculum could be that students in lower ability groups do not get the opportunity to mix with other students with differing abilities who may act as role models.

 Case study

Carl – grouping

Date, time, duration	Context	No ADHD	ADHD behaviours	
			Inattention	Hyperactivity/ Impulsivity
(i) Wed 25 Sep 11:00 – 60 minutes	**Literacy** – group, n = 4, working in withdrawal area – 6 varied activities, mainly oral.	88%	7%	5%

Date, time, duration	Context	No ADHD	ADHD behaviours	
			Inattention	Hyperactivity/ Impulsivity
(ii) Mon 30 Sep 09:17 – 50 minutes	**Numeracy** – group, n = 4, in withdrawal area with TA. Number bonds to 10; addition and subtraction games.	35%	21%	44%

Figure 5.6   Carl: grouping – extracts from fixed interval sampling observations

(i) Carl succeeded in sustaining attention for much of this well-planned group literacy lesson which was taken by the SENCO who worked with the (inexperienced) teaching assistant (TA) to offer support and suggestions for future working with the group. The lesson consisted of the following six short, varied activities which held the children's interest: recapping the story which they had started to read the previous day; taking turns to read a short section of the next part of the story (shared reading); answering the SENCO's questions about the story; discussing how and when to dial 999; role play around making an emergency call; and finally drawing an imaginary island and labelling specific features. There was a minimum of writing involved and this helped Carl who was always happy to offer ideas orally in the group but was less confident in his writing abilities. Throughout the lesson, either the SENCO or the TA kept Carl on task, offering individual support for most of the time.

(ii) In this numeracy lesson the same year Carl displayed his highest number of inattentive and hyperactive–impulsive behaviours. This was the first lesson on a Monday morning. The field notes include comments from the SENCO and TA regarding problems with Carl's behaviour on Monday mornings, following a weekend at home. There are also numerous references to Carl's repeated complaints that he 'did not like maths' and that he was 'no good' at maths. Many of the observation results show that he did not perform well in these lessons.

A small group setting does not always produce the same levels of 'No ADHD' behaviour in target students (see Carl's group numeracy lesson described above). In the majority of case studies numeracy lessons were delivered in small ability groups. As with literacy lessons these were regularly taken by teaching assistants in the cases of Carl and Adam. Overall the target students had difficulty in sustaining attention during numeracy lessons. Although individuals with ADHD are believed to experience difficulties with dyscalculia, there was some variation in the attitudes of the target students to numeracy lessons. Adam usually managed to pay attention, despite the fact that he often complained about numeracy lessons. Both Sanjay and Fergal performed better than their SEN peers in the numeracy groups. Carl and Edward actively disliked numeracy lessons and struggled with mathematical concepts, sense of time and sequencing, despite the extra support and encouragement provided in small groups. David did not show any positive dislike for the subject but displayed a high proportion of ADHD behaviours. It should be noted that, unlike non-ADHD students, those with ADHD may find that being taught different ways to find answers to mathematical questions can cause frustration and confusion.

Other small groups, such as Sanjay's speech and language group and Edward's additional literacy support group, produced higher levels of 'No ADHD' behaviour in target students. David and Fergal, the two target students who had experience of working in nurture groups, were observed to achieve higher levels of 'No ADHD' behaviour in these groups than in the main class settings. (The 'interventions' section in Chapter 1 provides further details on nurture groups.)

 Case study

Fergal – nurture group and main class setting

As can be seen in Figure 5.7 a lower proportion of ADHD behaviours was displayed by Fergal during the first year of the case study in the nurture group than in the main class setting. He displayed 11 per cent hyperactive–impulsive and 22 per cent inattentive behaviours in the nurture group and 19 per cent hyperactive–impulsive and 25 per cent inattention behaviours in the main class group. This led to correspondingly higher recordings for 'No ADHD' behaviours (67 per cent) in the nurture group compared to 56 per cent in the main class group.

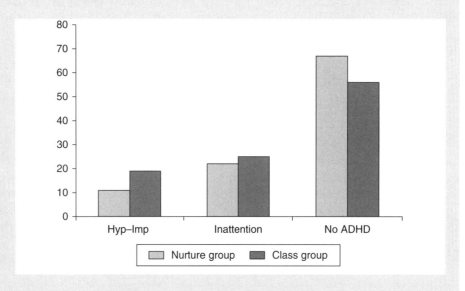

Figure 5.7 FIS recordings in nurture group and main class setting – Fergal

Fewer ADHD behaviours were also recorded for target students on occasions when one-to-one support was provided, as in the DT lessons highlighted earlier involving both Carl and David. Although this was usually adult support there were often examples of peer support (for example, as in the ICT lesson described above when David received support from John). There are occasions when peer support or peer tutoring may be used successfully as long as the teacher plans this carefully. When examining the effectiveness of one-to-one support for a student with ADHD, the quality of the relationship between the adult and the student is significant. A TA needs to know when to withdraw support, as for example in Carl's first science lesson described in Chapter 4. There was some reluctance on the part of three of the target students to 'share' a teaching assistant or special support assistant (SSA) with other students and there were concerns that Carl was becoming too dependent on his SSA. Relationships between students and teaching staff as well as the make-up of groups are important features which can affect the behaviour of individual students.

 Case study

Sanjay – grouping over time

As can be seen in Figure 5.8 there was a slight increase in the proportion of Sanjay's hyperactive–impulsive behaviours in the literacy group in the second year of the case study (from 12 to 13 per cent). There was a noticeable increase in inattentive behaviours (from 9 to 18 per cent), with the proportion of 'No ADHD' behaviours correspondingly lower in the second year of the case study (69 per cent) than in the first year (79 per cent). This may have been due in part to the relationships between Sanjay and his teachers. The group in the first year was taken by an experienced female SEN teacher whereas the group the following year was taken by a male teacher who often adopted a humorous approach in the lessons. Sanjay did not seem to understand the 'banter' that was often exchanged in lessons.

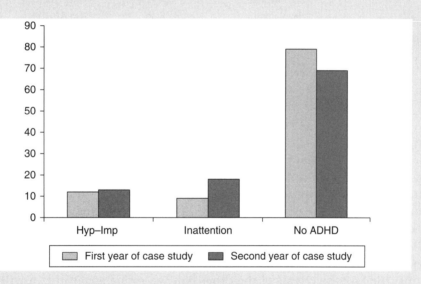

Figure 5.8   FIS recordings over time (literacy group) – Sanjay

The reverse to the above applied in Sanjay's 'No ADHD' figure for group numeracy lessons. This *increased* from 64 per cent in the first year to 73 per cent the following year (see Figure 5.9). Hyperactive–impulsive behaviours decreased significantly from 25 per cent to 11 per cent and inattentive behaviours increased from 11 per cent to 16 per cent. The numeracy group in the first year contained 15 students, several of whom displayed a variety of challenging behaviours. Although the same SEN teacher took both literacy and numeracy group lessons with a similar amount of support it was observed that in numeracy lessons there were often more distractions than

(Continued)

(Continued)

in literacy lessons. Following reports from the teacher to the SENCO, there was a change in the make-up of the group the following year. More of the students received individual adult support. Sanjay developed a particularly good relationship with the numeracy teacher and she saw his skills and confidence improve.

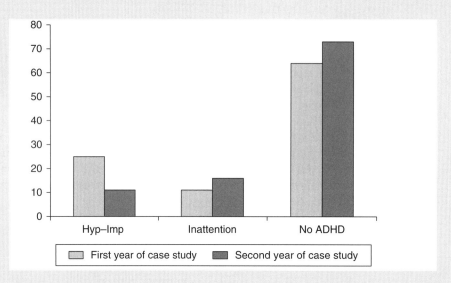

Figure 5.9   FIS recordings over time (numeracy group) – Sanjay

In the majority of schools any TA support in the classroom was generally in the mornings when literacy and numeracy lessons were taught, with a TA taking charge of teaching SEN groups in two schools. The class teacher often had no support in the whole-class lessons in the afternoons. Individuals with ADHD might benefit from extra support in whole-class lessons. These lessons could adopt different strategies including the teacher focusing on those students who need extra support and the TA overseeing the rest of the class. In Carl's DT lesson highlighted above the teacher worked with half the class on practical activities which needed particular support while the TA took charge of the other half who were engaged in a written activity. Carl's class was regularly divided into two once a week, as described in the extract from the music lesson in Chapter 4. The visiting music teacher took half of the class for music in the hall while the class teacher took the other half of the class for another activity (usually art). The two halves would then change over.

School training needs

In order for approaches such as those described in this chapter to be put into practice effectively there is a need for teacher education in this area, both at the initial teacher training stage and as part of continuing professional development, including INSET training. Informal interviews by the author found that there was interest among educational professionals in increasing their knowledge and expertise in managing

ADHD in the school situation. As mentioned in Chapter 3, staff in only 12 per cent of the schools responding to the ADHD survey indicated that they had received any relevant training, although the majority requested further training and support.

During the research period, the author was involved in organising and presenting at two ADHD study days entitled 'Including and Teaching Children with ADHD' (also mentioned in Chapter 3) which brought together professionals from education and health, psychologists, HE students, parents and support groups. For both study days, held on consecutive years at a university, each delegate was asked to complete an anonymous evaluation sheet identifying any outstanding questions or concerns on ADHD. These sheets were in three parts designed to elicit as much information as possible:

(A)   Before the programme started, delegates were asked to list up to three questions concerning ADHD that they would like to be addressed during the day's programme.

(B)   They were then invited to indicate at the end of the day how well each of the questions had been addressed. A five-point Likert-type scale was used ranging from 'excellently' to 'not at all'.

(C)   'Looking to the Future' – asked for the most pressing concerns about provision for the education of students with ADHD.

Detailed analyses of the evaluation sheets produced data that were used to supplement survey findings regarding local school training needs. At the first ADHD study day, held part-way through the data collection phase of the school survey, there were 107 completed sheets (61 per cent of delegates). The following year, when the survey results had been analysed and disseminated, there were 46 completed sheets (92 per cent). The highest percentage of the questions unanswered at the end of each day's programme focused on 'strategies' in both years (28 per cent the first year and 18 per cent the following year). This might indicate that the majority of the audiences were teachers and TAs who were interested in practical advice for coping with students with ADHD in the classroom. A wider number of issues were identified the second year, possibly due to increased awareness of the disorder.

The two highest percentages for 'most pressing concerns' show a similar pattern over the two years. Issues of 'provision, resources and support' were uppermost in the minds of delegates looking to the future. Interestingly, the percentage rose from 21 per cent at the first study day to 31 per cent the following year. The same applied to issues of 'awareness and understanding of ADHD', with a rise from 15 to 28 per cent. An increased emphasis on inclusive education and the publication of the Green Paper *Every Child Matters* (DfES, 2003) could account for this trend, together with an increase in knowledge and understanding of ADHD (Wheeler et al., 2008).

Although earlier chapters have provided general background information on ADHD, this chapter has sought to raise awareness of theories concerning the nature of the disorder in identifying effective teaching approaches based on findings from case study research. Chapter 6 offers an examination of how general classroom and behaviour management strategies can be used to benefit students with ADHD. It is to be hoped that 'teachers will find their own strategies once they understand the difficulties of these children' (Lovey, 1999: 183).

Points to remember

- The positive attributes of ADHD should be taken into account in curriculum planning.
- Educational practitioners should be aware of the theoretical background of ADHD when deciding on approaches for use with students who display ADHD symptoms.
- There should be flexibility in the delivery and organisation of the curriculum.
- A variety of teaching and learning styles is necessary.
- A range of grouping and support strategies should be adopted in the classroom.
- Effective training for educational practitioners in the implications of ADHD in the school setting is essential.

Questions for reflection and discussion

1. What difficulties do students with ADHD find in accessing the curriculum?
2. How can the delivery of the curriculum be modified to help individuals with ADHD?
3. Do you employ a variety of teaching and learning styles in lessons?
4. Are there any ways in which you can use different grouping and support strategies?
5. Do you feel confident in your knowledge of the concept and implications of ADHD?

6

Classroom and behaviour management strategies

Many of the general classroom and behaviour management strategies already in place in some schools may be appropriate in supporting students who display ADHD characteristics. The strategies and approaches described in this chapter, which are by no means all new or radical, could benefit many individuals in educational settings, not just those with a formal diagnosis of ADHD. By referring to DSM-IV criteria for ADHD, this chapter will highlight a range of general strategies aimed at reducing specific ADHD characteristics and behaviours in learners of all ages in inclusive classrooms. Checklists provide a wide selection of tried and tested ideas for you to implement. A short section focuses specifically on offering support to adolescents and suggestions are offered for whole-school characteristics which may benefit individuals with ADHD.

Classroom management strategies

The suggestions shown below are aimed at minimising ADHD-specific difficulties and increasing on-task behaviour in mainstream educational settings. Ideally a combination of proactive and reactive strategies should be adopted.

Inattention

The following approaches may be particularly useful for those students who are included in the 'predominantly inattentive' or 'combined' ADHD subtypes or who display behaviours included in the DSM-IV criteria for inattention (see Chapter 4 – fixed interval sampling and instantaneous time sampling observation schedules, behaviour categories 1–9). Students with the 'predominantly inattentive' subtype may easily be overlooked in a classroom as they tend not to draw attention to themselves in the same way as do those who display hyperactive–impulsive behaviours. Suggestions are examined in three areas: classroom layout, sustaining attention, and time management and organisation.

Classroom layout

Close attention should be paid to seating in the classroom which should preferably be self-contained rather than open-plan. In order to minimise distractions, an individual with ADHD or attention difficulties should be seated:

- close to the teacher;

- near to the front of the classroom with his back to other children;

- away from windows, doors, air conditioning and busy areas;

- near to good role models;

- with all unnecessary objects removed from desks;

- with a study carrel or screen around the desk on some occasions.

Ideally the student with ADHD will have the choice of two seats, one in a quiet place for times when he feels the need to remove himself from situations when he (or his teacher) feels he will not be able to cope with the distractions of the classroom and the other within a group to promote social contact and to encourage peer tutoring and cooperative learning.

 Case study

Edward – classroom arrangement

Edward had previously been known to wander out of the classroom when he found things difficult to cope with and the SENCO reported that there had been occasions in earlier years when he had tried to run away from school. The class teacher had very little TA support with a class of 30 students in the afternoons. It was arranged that if Edward felt he could not cope at any time in the main class group he should go and sit quietly in the book corner until he felt able to rejoin his classmates, which he did on several occasions when he appeared to be getting angry with himself or other children or frustrated with a particular task.

This meant that Edward had a quiet, safe place in which to calm down and that the teacher need not worry that he would leave the room unnoticed. It also ensured that his classmates could get on with their work without being distracted by Edward.

Sustaining attention

When organising classroom seating as detailed above, you should be able to move freely around the classroom and when necessary use an agreed signal, such as discreetly touching the student's desk in passing to remind him to stay focused or start on a task. The following suggestions may help the student with ADHD and also others in the class to sustain attention:

- Prime the student(s) before starting a task (how they will start, what will come next, what will be included).

- Break complicated tasks into manageable segments.

- Tasks should be stimulating and not repetitive.

- Where appropriate reduce task length.

- Use visual clues and reminders of what students should be doing.

- Follow a difficult task with a preferred task or a high-interest activity with a low-interest activity.

- Keep materials to hand.

- Differentiate learning materials.

- Worksheets should only include one or two activities/tasks; a simple page format should be used; avoid handwritten sheets; divide the page into sections so that the student can cover sections when they are not being used.

- Individuals with ADHD perform best working in a pair rather than a group – group situations can be overstimulating.

- Offer immediate and frequent feedback and as much reinforcement as possible.

- Ask students for their own ideas as to what strategies might help them.

Students with ADHD experience particular difficulties with understanding and following through instructions. These should be:

- given one at a time to avoid overwhelming the student;

- given clearly and frequently;

- repeated if necessary;

- broken into small chunks;

- clear and concise, with visual prompts accompanying verbal instructions.

It is important that when giving instructions you should:

- maintain eye contact;

- check the student has understood;

- ask the student to repeat back what is required;

- avoid signs of exasperation when repeating task requirements.

Listening to restful music can have benefits for all children, particularly those with ADHD, helping them to sustain attention, stay focused and work calmly when engaged in desk-based tasks. In some activities a learner with ADHD using headphones will be able to screen extraneous auditory stimuli and concentrate more easily on a task.

 Case study

Sanjay – use of background music, headphones

Sanjay's class usually split into ability groups for literacy lessons, but one day during the first year of the case study there was an unexpected change to routine and they remained in their class group. Following an introduction from the class teacher the children were required to make their own individual story books. As they were nearing the end of the lesson most had finished their written work and were drawing and colouring in pictures. The teacher put a story tape on the cassette player for the children to listen to as they worked. This is something the teacher often did in similar situations as she found that the class behaviour was improved on these occasions.

Individual headphones were also used in a phonics listening activity with a small sub-group in a group literacy lesson, which really helped Sanjay and his peers to concentrate for a longer period.

It is recommended that the flashcards included in Figure 6.1 (available as download-able materials) are 'personalised' so as to support particular difficulties experienced by individual students. They may be photocopied onto card and cut into individual flashcards. The student, with adult help where necessary, could be encouraged to draw and colour in a picture on the relevant flashcard of, for example, himself sitting on his chair or putting up his hand to answer a question. Alternatively the student could colour in a drawing provided by the adult. Cards may then be laminated for classroom use. Readers might choose to design their own cards using other phrases or illustrations to suit individual students or situations.

Time management and organisation
All students, particularly those displaying ADHD characteristics, benefit from the use of structure, routine, predictability and consistency in school settings (Kewley, 2005). Individuals with ADHD have problems with the concept of time and time management and they find change difficult to deal with. Due to poor short-term memory they are forgetful, often needing help in organising themselves and in planning activities or tasks. The following suggestions can help in minimising some of these difficulties and also in developing self-management techniques.

- Establish uncomplicated daily and weekly class routines.

- Have a timetable clearly on display in the classroom as well as providing individual copies. Younger learners will benefit from a visual timetable and it is useful if this is explained at the start of the day, morning or afternoon.

I put up my hand	**I can stand in line**
I sit on my chair	**Stop ... think ... answer**

Figure 6.1 Classroom flashcards

(Continued)

(Continued)

I stay in my seat	**I get straight down to work**
I remember to take turns	**I do not call out answers**

- If possible, there should be warnings of any changes.

- Provide the individual with a flashcard 'I get straight down to work' (Figure 6.1).

- Individual whiteboards can be useful in primary classrooms to list the tasks required. Students can tick off each task as it is completed. Older learners could use a highlighter or cross off items on a written list.

- Encourage the use of 'brainstorming' or 'mind-mapping' sheets for assignments.

- Use timers to help in self-pacing – depending on the age of the student, these can range from simple sand timers to cooker timers or battery-operated timers with different coloured sections and different sounds to indicate the time allotted.

- Allow students to use highlighters and sticky notes for prioritising tasks or as reminders for what needs to be done during a specific time period.

- Develop a clear system for keeping track of completed/uncompleted work.

- Use humorous mnemonics to assist memorising (O'Regan, 2002).

- Arrange peer support where appropriate.

- Where possible, enlist help from home – for example, if a student often forgets his PE kit or homework – or offer further support in school.

 Case study

Edward – forgetfulness

Edward repeatedly forgot to bring his PE kit into school and unfortunately the school had not been successful in gaining cooperation from home. The class teacher made a point of keeping a spare kit so that Edward was able to take part in PE lessons. Other students who occasionally forgot their kit may have had to sit out the lesson if there was not enough spare kit but the teacher felt that it was important for Edward not to miss out on these lessons, for two main reasons:

1. So that he had the chance of taking part in some physical activity. He may have found it difficult to sit still on a bench in the gym while his classmates took part in their PE lesson.
2. To provide him with opportunities for cooperation and turn-taking in lessons which included some form of teamwork. For example, during an intra-school sports day Edward was included in a mixed-age team who took part in various sporting activities in the school hall. When he seemed to be having difficulty in following through instructions his team-mates would encourage him and tell him what to do.

Hyperactive–impulsive

Students diagnosed with the 'hyperactive–impulsive' or 'combined' subtypes of ADHD or those who display any of the DSM-IV criteria for 'hyperactivity' (10–15) and/or any of the 'impulsivity' criteria (16–18) (see FIS and ITS observation schedules in Chapter 4) can often cause the most disruption in school settings.

Hyperactivity

There are varying degrees of hyperactivity (both motor and verbal) and many individuals with ADHD become less hyperactive as they get older. Motor hyperactivity includes high levels of fidgeting, unauthorised movement in the classroom and an inability to play or engage in leisure activities quietly. Early years and primary school class management offers more opportunities for a child to move around the classroom. Secondary and high school students are not able to roam around so easily in classroom settings, although there is more movement involved between lessons. Students displaying verbal hyperactivity are often noisy and over-talkative compared with their peers. The following strategies can help reduce hyperactive behaviours.

- Allow students to use a doodle pad, a piece of Blu-tack or other stress toy to keep their hands occupied, for example in a primary setting when the class sit on the carpet for the teacher's instructions for a task.

- Seating arrangements have been mentioned earlier, but it is also useful to allow an individual to stand at times when working.

- Give the student a flashcard such as 'I stay in my seat' or 'I sit on my chair' (see Figure 6.1).

- Allow the individual to take 'seat breaks' – plan opportunities for productive physical movement (for example, handing out books or running errands).

- Increase opportunities for on-task verbal participation.

- Use a flashcard 'I can stand in line' (Figure 6.1) as a reminder.

- Coordinate and plan movement around the school.

- Use a range of peer mentoring approaches to offer support in situations such as moving around the school, sitting in a large school hall and working/playing cooperatively with other pupils.

Impulsiveness

Students with ADHD often blurt out answers, experience difficulty in waiting their turn and interrupt others. They may display some or all of the following three types of impulsive behaviour which can lead to difficulties not only in the *cognitive* domain, having an effect on academic achievement, but also in the *affective* domain, which includes emotional and social difficulties. (These are examined in more detail in Chapter 7.)

- *Physical impulsiveness* – where individuals act without forethought, having no idea of cause and effect, often putting themselves in danger.

- *Verbal impulsiveness* – where students shout out in class, either when they are keen to give a correct answer or often even when they do not know the correct answer. They also often feel the need to say out loud something that is on their mind, even if it is unconnected with the lesson. They interrupt conversations much more often than non-ADHD students and may say hurtful things to their peers without appreciating the effect they may have.

- *Emotional impulsiveness* – where individuals have marked mood swings and temper outbursts, often for little or no reason (Kewley, 2005).

 Case study

Adam – impulsiveness

On one occasion Adam ran across the school car park chasing a football out towards the main road. Luckily a workman employed near to the school saw him and retrieved the ball for him. Adam's mother was informed of the school's concerns. Instead of making him lose playtimes, he was banned from playing football for the time being, but was still allowed out to play. This meant that he could still get some physical exercise by running around and playing on the adventure playground with his friends.

The suggestions shown below may help to minimise impulsive behaviour.

- Provide individual flashcards such as 'I put up my hand', 'Stop … think … answer' or 'I do not call out answers' (Figure 6.1). These should be changed from time to time.

- Young learners sitting on the carpet for a lesson or teacher's instructions might benefit from a TA sitting at the front of the group holding up a large coloured cut-out picture of a hand outline on a stick. This will be clearly visible throughout the session and will silently remind students to put up their hand before answering (Uniview, 2003).

- Students can use individual whiteboards on which to write their answers. These can be quietly held up and shown to the teacher.

- Use a variety of visual clues and reminders of what students should be doing.

- Use a flashcard 'I remember to take turns' (Figure 6.1).

- Limit the amount of time-waiting wherever possible.

- For those students experiencing difficulty waiting their turn, provide individual glue sticks or textbooks so that students do not have to share with others.

- Use 'Circle time' activities and game-playing to reinforce turn-taking.

- Ignore inappropriate comments where possible. Provide positive reinforcement for listening.

- Encourage students to write down or draw their thoughts and ideas to put into a box for the teacher to read later on.

Behaviour management strategies

Individuals with ADHD experience difficulties with behaviour inhibition and rule-governed behaviour. They 'struggle in environments that demand restraint, goal-directed actions, single-mindedness of purpose, self-regulation and ... delayed gratification' (Barkley, in DuPaul and Stoner, 2003: ix–x). The following suggestions can be useful in supporting all students, especially those with ADHD.

- Rules should be consistent, positive, clearly displayed and referred to. (If possible, they should be drawn up by the class and teacher at the beginning of each term.)

- Remain calm and do not shout.

- Involve the students in deciding rewards and sanctions.

- Model appropriate behaviour at all times.

- Value good behaviour by rewarding it and withdraw rewards for undesirable behaviour.

- Use a variety of simple behavioural interventions such as time-out, ignore-rules-praise (where rule-breaking behaviour is ignored and rule-complaint behaviour is praised), behavioural contracts and token economies (where rewards are given for positive rule-complaint behaviour) (Cooper and Bilton, 2002). These should be changed or modified from time to time.

- Positive behaviour-related comments should be made four times as often as negative comments (Spohrer, 2002).

- Any reprimands should be short and given at the time of the incident. Tell students what is expected as part of the reprimand.

- Do not keep a student with ADHD in at playtimes – not only does this deprive the learner of the opportunity for physical exercise but also limits opportunities for social learning.

- Where possible positive instructions should be used, such as 'Put your feet on the floor' rather than 'Don't put your feet on the desk'.

Adolescents

The transition from primary to secondary school is much more difficult for students with ADHD than it is for their peers. They are expected to be more autonomous and organised and there is often less individual support available for them than they may have been used to in a smaller primary school setting.

 Case study

David – school transition

Supportive relationships had been built up between David and members of the teaching staff in his first school. At the age of 9 years he attended a learning support base twice a week for hourly literacy lessons where he worked in a group of six or seven students with the SENCO and a TA. He also attended twice-weekly nurture group sessions, which took place in the same classroom with the same teaching staff.

In David's large middle school the following year some lessons were taken by the registration class teacher and others by specialist teachers. Students moved between classrooms in a manner more often found in a secondary school.

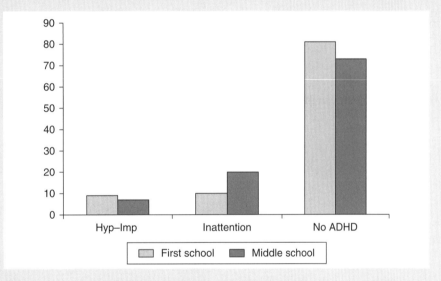

Figure 6.2 FIS recordings over time, all settings – David

Figure 6.2 shows that the proportion of 'hyperactive–impulsive' behaviours displayed by David decreased slightly from 9 per cent in the first school to 7 per cent in the middle school. However, 'inattention' behaviours rose significantly from 10 to 20 per cent and 'No ADHD' figures fell from 81 to 73 per cent. Although other factors might have affected his behaviour, this analysis of the observation data indicates that David displayed more ADHD behaviours in the middle school than in the first school setting.

Suggested strategies for use with adolescents

Most of the strategies suggested in the above sections on classroom and behaviour management are suitable for students of all ages. However, some will require modification when used with students in secondary or high schools where there are different challenges and demands. For example, instead of using flashcards as shown in Figure 6.1, smaller individual cards without pictures could be used. Lovey (1999) describes the use of laminated cards, the size of a credit card, bearing the word 'REMEMBER!' By carrying such a card with them in school from classroom to classroom the student can discreetly place it on their desk. This has two benefits:

- It will act as a visual reminder to the student to concentrate, to check each piece of work and not to shout out.

- Particularly in a large secondary school when teachers might only see some children once a week, it will remind each teacher to keep an eye on the student to ensure he or she remains on-task.

Listed below are several areas in which adolescents who display ADHD behaviour may need particular support in school. The suggestions, taken from a larger discussion of strategies by Robin (1998), may not be possible or appropriate in all schools with all students.

Homework

- Where possible, shorten homework assignments.

- Assign a peer for each class to remind the learner to write down assignments in a daily assignment book.

- Allow more time for assignments.

- Provide a set of textbooks for use at home.

Test-taking

- Permit extra time during tests.

- Arrange for the student to take the test in a non-distracting environment.

- Arrange for oral or alternative methods of testing competence.

- Permit short breaks during tests.

- Use quizzes instead of longer tests.

Reading comprehension

- Provide books on tape.

- Provide the student with a written outline of the chapters.

- Highlight main ideas in the text.

- Substitute easier texts on the same topic.

Lesson presentation/note-taking

- Slow down the rate of presentation of a lesson.

- Repeat and summarise information often.

- Emphasise key points for note-taking – write these on the board.

- Give permission to tape-record the lesson.

- Allow a laptop computer for note-taking.

- Allow a teaching assistant to take notes on behalf of the student.

Whole-school characteristics

The delivery and organisation of the curriculum can be unique to each class, teacher and school. The ethos and policies of a school are important and the following list of school characteristics may benefit individuals with ADHD (Cooper and Bilton, 2002; Kewley, 2005):

- teacher consultation on school management and curricular issues;

- sharing of pastoral and academic responsibilities between staff;

- timetabling lessons requiring high levels of cognitive engagement earlier rather than later in the day;

- effective systems for protecting and nurturing students' self-esteem;

- consistent arrangements for rewards and sanctions;

- a good extra-curricular programme where children can develop their strengths away from their academic studies;

- student consultation on school management and curricular issues;

- positive parental involvement;

- effective multi-agency cooperation;

- all teaching and non-teaching staff, including lunchtime supervisors and administration staff, having an understanding of the nature of ADHD and its implications;

- appropriate INSET training so that teachers can increase their knowledge and expertise in managing ADHD in the school situation.

Although aimed particularly at individuals who display ADHD behaviours, the strategies and ideas highlighted in this chapter may be of benefit to all students.

Most are inexpensive and do not involve too much organising or disruption and the teacher is not required to use different strategies for different groups of students. The focus here has been on aiming to reduce specific ADHD characteristics as outlined in DSM-IV criteria. Chapter 7 will go on to examine some of the other difficulties associated with the disorder.

 Points to remember

- Many of the classroom and behaviour management strategies already used by some teachers are suitable for learners who display ADHD behaviours.
- Approaches recommended for students with ADHD may be beneficial for all students.
- A whole-school approach is important in supporting learners who display ADHD behaviours.

 Questions for reflection and discussion

1. What can be done in classrooms to support students who display ADHD characteristics?
2. How would any changes affect other students?
3. What could be improved at school level?

 Remember: The classroom flashcards (Figure 6.1) are also available from www. sagepub.co.uk/wheeler.

7

Associated and coexisting difficulties

Chapter 5 has examined observed variability in ADHD behaviours to identify effective teaching approaches for individuals with ADHD and Chapter 6 has highlighted general classroom strategies which may be useful in reducing ADHD behaviours included in the three core symptoms of inattention, hyperactivity and impulsivity (APA, 2000). By drawing on research findings and other literature this final chapter in Section 2 aims to raise awareness of some of the cognitive, affective and other difficulties associated with ADHD which may provide further challenges for the student and the teacher in the school environment. Where possible suggestions are made as to how some of these difficulties may be alleviated.

Findings from the school survey concur with published suggestions that 70 per cent of students with ADHD experience coexisting or comorbid conditions. Figure 7.1 offers a breakdown of 'other SEN' reported in the 413 students with a diagnosis of ADHD in a local authority. It can be seen that the highest number of students experienced emotional and behavioural difficulties (EBD), with the second highest proportion reported as experiencing general learning difficulties. The figures also show that there is evidence of 'multiple comorbidity', that is the simultaneous existence of two or more different conditions.

Description of SEN	Number of students
Emotional and behavioural difficulties	189
Learning difficulties (general)	112
Speech and language difficulties	49
Autistic spectrum disorder	40
Specific learning difficulties	39
Physical disabilities	15
Sensory difficulties	10
Total	454*

Figure 7.1 Description of other SEN reported in students diagnosed with ADHD

*Includes multiple comorbidity

Cognitive difficulties

Many of the difficulties associated with ADHD can prevent individuals from achieving academically. In the school survey 47 per cent of students diagnosed with ADHD were reported as not achieving educationally at their age level. This may be an underestimate as 23 per cent of recordings were 'not known' or not provided. The six target students in the case studies experienced general learning difficulties. Carl was reported in the survey as having specific learning difficulties and a Statement of SEN focusing on his learning difficulties was issued in his final year in primary school. All target students had problems with basic literacy and numeracy skills, speech and language development, mathematical concepts and sequences, and time management and sense of time.

Basic literacy difficulties, particularly in reading and language processing, may affect other areas of the curriculum and school life. The target students were often unable to read the words of hymns from hymn books or overhead projector screens in assemblies. This added to their inability to focus when in the school hall and led to higher numbers of ADHD behaviours being displayed. On several occasions the target students needed peer support in the reading of instructions, for example on a computer screen, as in David's ICT lesson highlighted in Chapter 5. The following extracts demonstrate how literacy difficulties experienced by Adam and David affected their academic achievement in mathematics.

 Case studies: literacy difficulties

Adam

During the second year of the case study Adam's numeracy group were having a short test. The TA wrote seven questions on the board and stressed that the children must work in silence to get used to the idea of working under test conditions. Adam called out: *'I can't do number 6 ... Don't know what **rounded** means. Can you tell me what it is?'*

The TA replied: *'No, because this is a test. I'll tell you afterwards. Miss that one out and go on to the next one.'*

Later when they were going over the answers the TA asked the group: *'What is 83 rounded to the nearest 10?'*

After Adam had made a wild guess and called out *'39'* the TA went on to explain the meaning of **rounded** to the group.

David

A teacher's note included in school records consulted during the case study refers explicitly to David's mathematics test scores being affected by his poor reading skills at ages 7, 8 and 9 years. It was clear that David was aware of his reading problems. At the beginning of a numeracy lesson during the first year of the case study when the teacher was writing problem-solving questions on the board, David kept calling out: *'I can't read it ... I can't do them ... I can't read them ... I'm not good at reading ... Miss, I have problems with my reading ...'*

Testing

Students with ADHD and associated cognitive difficulties do not perform well in tests such as Standard Assessments Tasks (SATs) (used in England – see Chapter 9) or similar tests which rely on their ability to express their knowledge and understanding of subjects in written answers under time-limited examination conditions. All six target students attained lower than expected levels in SATs and other non-statutory tests.

As students progress through school there are more tests and exams which can present challenges to both students and teachers. Examinations often 'involve a large number of coursework assignments, over which it is all too easy for those with ADHD to procrastinate, and the exams require them to plan ahead and to concentrate on subjects that they may not find interesting' (Kewley, 2005: 21). It is to be hoped that the recent introduction of Diplomas for some 14–19 year olds which combine theoretical study with practical experience might offer support for older students who experience difficulties associated with ADHD (DCSF, 2008).

Affective difficulties

In addition to cognitive teaching and learning there is a need for increased emphasis on the affective curriculum (sometimes referred to as the 'hidden' curriculum) in schools as individuals with ADHD often experience significant difficulties in this domain. Over 50 per cent are reported as displaying emotional and social skills problems (Cooper and Bilton, 2002). The six target students in the case studies suffered from a range of emotional and behavioural difficulties. Fergal's problems were reported as 'severe' and he was the only target student to be issued with a Statement of SEN which included a mention of his complex range of challenging behaviours. Three main areas of affective difficulties – emotional immaturity, problems with social relationships and poor self-esteem – are interlinked and are discussed below.

Emotional immaturity

All six target students appeared to be more emotionally immature than their peers. These findings concur with the suggestion by Green and Chee that individuals with ADHD have the 'social and emotional maturity of a child two-thirds their age' (1997: 6). They were often observed putting fingers in their mouths or sucking or chewing pencil cases or other classroom equipment.

 Case studies

Emotional immaturity

As highlighted in Chapter 5, *Fergal* displayed fewer ADHD symptoms when in the nurture group in the first year of the case study and he seemed to experience difficulty in changing from the emotionally supportive environment of the nurture group to the main class group. In both years he was observed to be almost constantly sucking his thumb or chewing his sweatshirt cuffs, plastic water bottle, pencil case, pens and pencils. He could be over-emotional at times

(Continued)

(Continued)

and started crying when disappointed with his test results in a numeracy lesson during the second year of the case study.

Edward and *Adam* also often became upset and cried more easily than their peers. For example, in a numeracy group lesson *Adam* did not get all his sums right and cried because he did not get a sweet. Both *Fergal* and *Edward* brought in small toys from home. A lack of appropriate inhibition was observed on occasions when *Edward, Fergal* and *Adam* hugged adults. *Edward* was also observed touching and, occasionally, kissing peers inappropriately.

There were many examples of anxiety symptoms displayed by *David* during both years of the case study. He was often seen with his fingers or the sleeve of his sweatshirt in his mouth. He continually sought praise and reassurance from adults, often getting up from his seat to take his work over to show the teacher or TA.

Social relationships

Findings from a sociometric question ('Which two children would you choose to play with in the school playground?') posed by the researcher in the case study research to target students and their classmates show that those with ADHD were not chosen as playmates. This finding is in line with studies employing sociometric measures which have found high rates of peer rejection for children displaying ADHD-related behaviours (DuPaul and Stoner, 2003). Throughout the case studies there were examples of students not wanting to sit next to target students or being reluctant to choose them as partners in activities in the classroom or in lessons such as PE. It is essential that learners of all ages are taught acceptance of those with ADHD and understanding of the difficulties they may experience. In addition to social skills training in the school context, after-school clubs or other activities run by voluntary agencies may provide opportunities for those with ADHD to excel at something and make friends.

 Case studies

Social relationships

The target students experienced varying degrees of social relationship problems, often seeming 'out of step with the chronological age of their development' (O'Regan, 2002: 27). Four of the six received some form of extra social skills training in school.

Sanjay was often clumsy and occasionally aggressive towards his peers. He made slight progress following the efforts of his teacher during the first year of the case study to pair him with a 'buddy' at playtimes. Sanjay attended after-school clubs for football and computers.

Carl preferred to play with younger children. At playtimes during both years of the case study he was often seen playing with a group of girls and, whenever the opportunity arose, he appeared much happier talking to an adult. In the second year he attended the after-school computer club and helped the SENCO to take after-school cookery classes for the younger students.

David appeared to be timid and not sure how to interact with his peers. He was always happy to speak to adults, whether it was to ask for help or for a more general conversation. On one occasion when he was aged 9 years, groups of students aged 5–7 years and 7–11 years came together to play simple board games and he worked well with the younger children.

Edward preferred to play with girls, choosing the same two girls as playmates in answer to the sociometric question for both years of the case study. There are several references in the field notes to his lack of the social skills necessary to make friendships. It was clear that his classmates seemed to accept that he needed to go and sit in the book corner on some occasions (as mentioned previously) and no one made a fuss or drew attention to him.

Fergal had difficulty playing appropriately with his peers and often became aggressive towards others. During the second year of the case study he was assigned a TA to accompany him for lunchtimes and playtimes to try to encourage social skills.

Adam had poor social skills and found it difficult to make friends. When observed playing football at playtimes he did not appear to be interested in social interaction, preferring instead to dominate the game.

Individuals with ADHD often have difficulties with initiating and maintaining friendships and they need to be taught some of the basic skills of social interaction. Their impulsiveness might lead them to interrupt conversations and to intrude upon or butt in to other students' games. They find it difficult to take turns and to empathise with others and often lack understanding of social rules. Consequently they may say upsetting or tactless things to their peers without realising the effect they may have. Flashcards such as 'I remember to take turns' (see Figure 6.1), previously suggested to help minimise impulsive behaviour in the classroom, might be useful in encouraging social and friendship skills in young students. Parents of students with ADHD are often more concerned with how well their child is able to socialise than with academic achievement (O'Regan, 2002). Other parents with limited knowledge of ADHD may perceive individuals with ADHD as unsuitable friends for their children.

 ## Case study

Sanjay – peer rejection

During the first year of the case study, at the end of a day of activities held for students from several schools in a local church, the following note was recorded by the researcher: 'No one chose Sanjay as their partner to sit with on the coach. George was the only other boy without a partner and he reluctantly sat with him.'

Also, when sitting in the church, Sanjay had told the researcher that he was looking round for his friend among another school group, saying *'He lives by me. I live at number 1 and he's number 3, but his Mom won't let him play with me.'*

During an informal interview following parents' evening, Sanjay's class teacher said that his parents were pleased with his progress but were still worried about peer acceptance. He had been excited recently when he received his first party invitation. A girl in his class was having a 'Disco' birthday party which meant she was able to invite a large number of children.

One of Sanjay's previous class teachers told the researcher that the perceptions of the other parents had often been a problem. In his first two years at school Sanjay had acquired 'a bad name'. A big boy for his age, he was clumsy and often frightened his peers in his attempts to befriend them.

I can tell someone likes me ....
....
....

.... is a good friend. Something we like
to do together is ....
....

Figure 7.2 'Friendship' worksheets

Previous research carried out several years ago by the author with students aged 6–7 years has successfully utilised worksheets such as those in Figure 7.2 (also available as downloadable material) in helping to improve friendship skills. A small group of students would be taken to a withdrawal area and following various activities such as the use of finger puppets, role play, games and the reading and discussion of relevant stories, the children would draw and colour in a picture and complete one or two sentences on one or other of the worksheets (Wheeler, 1996). Alternatively students could cut out suitable pictures from magazines or catalogues and stick these onto the worksheets. Personal, Social and Health Education (PSHE) lessons, circle time activities, role play and drama can be useful in teaching concepts of communication, participation and cooperation. Topics for circle time can be chosen bearing in mind the particular needs of an individual with ADHD.

 Case study

Fergal – circle time

During a circle time session observed in Fergal's nurture group the focus was on 'giving a compliment' and 'what makes me happy'. Following the teacher's introduction a soft toy was passed around and the student holding it was allowed to speak while the others listened. A girl in the group said: *'When Fergal plays nicely, I feel happy'.* When it was Fergal's turn he addressed the TA (Mrs T), saying: *'When Mrs T smiles, she makes everyone happy'.* Throughout the session the TA sat next to Fergal and offered him plenty of support to help him sustain attention.

Fergal had been known to be very aggressive in the playground and was often involved in fights. Towards the end of the session (the last of the morning, followed by lunch and playtime) the teacher referred to playground behaviour and reminded the group about using 'gentle touches' when playing with friends.

The following suggestions from Holowenko (1999) could prove useful in social skills training for students with difficulties associated with ADHD. These skills should be taught within the context of the whole class.

- Build a 'Circle of Friends' or buddy support system.

- Teach conflict resolution strategies or assertiveness for all students.

- Use flexible groupings to ensure that children with ADHD work with a variety of children.

- Peer tutoring or spelling partners should be monitored and rotated.

- Encourage seeing situations from another's viewpoint.

- Model appropriate social skills.

- Foster the ethos that everyone is a worthwhile member of the group.

Self-esteem

There are references in the literature to poor self-esteem among individuals with a diagnosis of ADHD. 'Many behaviours associated with ADHD may have a significant impact on a child's self-esteem. Protecting and enhancing it through the school years is a crucial goal of effective management' (Kewley, 2005: 71). A concept such as self-esteem is difficult to measure or assess. 'Measurement' implies a quantitative process, but self-esteem is a set of attitudes and part of an individual's personality which cannot be observed directly. The primary version of the 'LAWSEQ' student questionnaire, in which a maximum 'score' of 24 is possible (Lawrence, 1996), had been successfully employed alongside qualitative techniques in previous research with 6–7 year old students (Wheeler, 1996). A decision was made to use an adaptation of this in the case studies in an attempt to reach some conclusions regarding the self-esteem of the target students in relation to their peers. In most cases the LAWSEQ findings agreed with opinions formed following observations made by the researcher and discussed with teaching staff.

 Case studies

Self-esteem

Sanjay appeared to have a high self-esteem compared to the majority of his classmates, with only slight variability over time. His scores during both years of the case study were higher than the class average, with his score of 21 the first year being joint second highest in the class.

Carl did not appear to suffer from poor self-esteem, scoring around the class average, with only slight variability over time.

Although it is difficult to draw any conclusions regarding ***David***'s level of self-esteem which was below the class average, it appears to have remained stable over the school transition and over time.

There appeared to be some variability in ***Edward***'s level of self-esteem over the two years of the study. During the first year his self-esteem score was marginally above the class average. The following year his score decreased to below the class average.

Fergal's move from first school to middle school meant that self-esteem questionnaires were administered to different cohorts in the main and follow-up phases. His levels of self-esteem appeared to vary over time, but were below the class average.

Adam's level of self-esteem appeared to show the greatest increase over time from 12 (well below the class average) to 17 out of a possible 24.

The self-esteem findings from the case study research imply that the target students' scores do not generally concur with suggestions of poor self-esteem in individuals with ADHD. It is difficult to draw any conclusions from the results of the questionnaires but it does appear that the self-esteem 'scores' for both Carl and Adam increased in the second year of the case studies. There could be any number of reasons for this including sampling fluctuations, but it is interesting to note that in both cases there was an increase in the percentage of 'No ADHD' behaviours recorded using the fixed interval sampling observation technique (Carl's figure increased from 61 to 71 per cent and Adam's from 65 to 73 per cent). Carl had started to receive extra classroom support following the issuing of a Statement of SEN and Adam had been diagnosed with ADHD and had begun taking medication.

Extracts in previous chapters have highlighted lessons where Carl was provided with opportunities to boost his self-esteem by sharing his innovative ideas with his peers in science and design and technology lessons. Activities employed in the author's previous research in enhancing the self-esteem of students were used alongside those mentioned above for improving friendship skills and include the following:

- a range of activities aimed at reinforcing feelings of identity and uniqueness – including work on 'names', their origins and meanings and making 'Name Collages';

- games using 'Feelings' dice – depicting six different feelings, for example *happy, sad, proud, scared, angry, excited,* to encourage students to talk about their feelings;

- making and using 'sad' and 'happy' face masks and various finger puppets to help students overcome their inhibitions when discussing their feelings;

- games and discussions using a set of cards on which are printed 'friendly/ unfriendly' statements and another set with short phrases detailing situations which could cover a range of emotions or feelings;

- the use of weekly worksheets with outlines of five or seven 'Feeling Good' banners providing spaces in which students write a positive thing each day that they (or someone else) may have done or said which has made them feel better about themselves (Figure 7.3, also available as downloadable material) (Wheeler, 1996).

The activities described above are all inexpensive and with the range of graphics and drawing programmes available on the computers of today they could easily be designed for use with younger or older students. For example, the 'Feeling Good' banners could be enlarged or modified using pictures of kites or balloons so that there is room for younger learners to draw pictures rather than writing. The 'Feelings' dice could have pictures or a combination of pictures and words to depict feelings. There are also numerous published suggestions for self-esteem enhancing activities, some specifically aimed at individuals with ADHD and other more general suggestions for all students which could also be appropriate (see the suggestions for further reading at the end of this book). The whole class could benefit from activities which may help

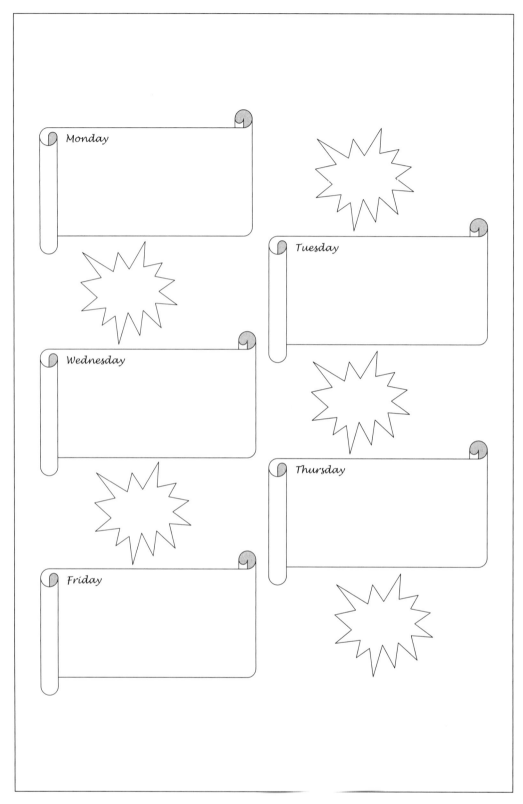

Figure 7.3 'Feeling Good' banners

to improve their self-esteem and, as with the suggestions in the previous chapter for behaviour and classroom management, the teacher can adopt the same activities for all students.

Social and emotional aspects of learning (SEAL)

As part of the National Strategies in the UK a voluntary whole-school programme known as SEAL (social and emotional aspects of learning) has been developed to promote social and emotional skills across the curriculum, initially with learners aged 3–11 years and more recently in secondary schools. The programme focuses on the five following social and emotional aspects of learning:

- self-awareness

- empathy

- managing feelings

- motivation

- social skills.

There are several sets of SEAL materials aimed at delivering seven whole-school themes: one set for teachers; colour-coded sets for use with different year groups; a set for use in small groups with students who may need additional help in developing their social, emotional and behavioural skills; and a set including additional activities for families to use at home (DfES, 2005). Even if schools choose not to implement the SEAL programme, some of the ideas may be incorporated into any school curriculum planning and added to work already being undertaken in the development of social, emotional and behavioural skills which could benefit students with affective difficulties associated with ADHD.

Other difficulties

Chapter 1 has provided a list of some of the coexisting problems associated with ADHD. Further details are provided here of some of the more common difficulties observed during the case study research.

Handwriting

Cooper and Bilton (2002) refer to US research findings which report that 60 per cent of children with ADHD have serious handwriting difficulties. The six target students experienced problems with fine motor control which led to problems with dressing and tying shoelaces as well as handwriting difficulties.

> Handwriting is a complicated learning task: the child has to have mastered certain levels of visual-perception, visual motor, gross and fine motor skills … [and should also be able to] pay attention and learn the skills as taught by the teacher.

The Three Ps of handwriting:

Posture ... good posture provides the stability to the child's body that can allow the mobility of the hand ...
Paper ... needs to be positioned correctly so that the child can see what he or she is writing.
Pencil/pen ... needs to be a good quality tool that works for the child ... (Kewley, 2005: 73–4)

The following suggested strategies, some of which were identified in the case studies, may also be suitable for use with students who experience handwriting difficulties:

- TA or other student to act as note-taker.

- Allow the student to dictate answers.

- Modify the amount of writing required by differentiating worksheets.

- Use other forms of recording, for example drawings and pictures.

- Use a computer or word processor.

- Use speech-enabled software.

- Include kinaesthetic approaches to teaching handwriting.

- Use different pens, grips.

- Provide occupational therapy support.

Oversensitivity

Children and young people with ADHD are often very sensitive to touch, smell, noise and a wide range of other stimuli. Some may be unduly affected by cold and warmth, with higher temperatures reported as possibly influencing neurotransmitter levels. An awareness of these sensitivities can be very important in the management of these children. Types of fabric, labels on clothes, subtle smells and minor changes in their environment may not be well tolerated (Kewley, 1999).

 Case studies

Oversensitivity

The field notes include several references to **Sanjay's** dislike of loud noises. The following extract was recorded during a special concert in which a high-school band played in the school hall:

10:53 Song is played (very loudly) ... Sanjay seems a bit bemused by it all.

11:17 Puts fingers in ears briefly ... Looking round the hall at other children who are clapping.

It was apparent on several occasions that *Carl* disliked loud noises. On a trip to the theatre during the first year of the case study the researcher sat next to him and wrote later:

> Carl didn't join in audience participation. Not sure if he was happy with all the noise. He preferred chatting quietly to researcher about the play and the new *Harry Potter* film he had seen recently.

There are several instances recorded when Carl did not seem to like tight clothes around him or that he felt hot. He would sometimes remove his sweatshirt or untuck his shirt so that he could flap it and get some cool air on his skin.

Edward appeared hypersensitive to loud noises. There are also several references to his being the only student in class to take off his sweatshirt, complaining he was too hot.

Further difficulties

There is a higher likelihood of sleeping problems in children with ADHD than in non-ADHD children. These may include difficulties with time taken to fall asleep, frequent night waking and tiredness on awakening (Barkley, 2006). Carl was the only target student identified as having sleep problems, for which he was prescribed melatonin. Edward and Fergal rarely smiled and were heard to make several inappropriate references to death and dying. There are references in the cases of Edward and Adam to the possible adverse effects of food additives (E numbers) on levels of hyperactivity. In addition to the difficulties discussed in this chapter and mentioned in Chapter 1, Kewley (2005) highlights the following common problems for adolescents with ADHD: oppositionality, conduct disorder, anxiety and depression, frustration, demotivation, the need for stimulation, drug and alcohol abuse, accidents, teenage pregnancy and suicide.

The four chapters in Section 2 have focused specifically on the school setting. The third and final section will examine factors in the wider context, beginning with Chapter 8 which focuses on the importance of parental involvement in children's education.

Points to remember

- Seventy per cent of students with ADHD may experience a range of coexisting or comorbid conditions.
- Basic literacy difficulties may affect academic achievement in other curriculum areas.
- Attention should be paid to the affective curriculum in schools.
- Individuals with ADHD appear to be more emotionally immature than their peers.
- There is a need for social skills training for students with ADHD.
- Some students with ADHD may suffer from poor self-esteem.

Questions for reflection and discussion

1. Do you feel you have sufficient awareness of comorbid conditions and associated difficulties likely to be experienced by students with ADHD?
2. In what ways could you/your school improve the social skills of students with ADHD?
3. Are you familiar with SEAL? Do you think it is a useful resource?

Remember: The 'Friendship' worksheets (Figure 7.2) and 'Feeling Good' banners (Figure 7.3) are also available from www.sagepub.co.uk/wheeler.

Section 3

The Wider Context

8

Working with parents

> The previous section has focused in detail on the school setting, but what happens in school does not occur in isolation. People and events outside the school environment are likely to have an effect on the learning and behaviour of students, particularly those displaying ADHD characteristics. The third and final section will examine factors in the wider context, beginning in this chapter by focusing on the importance of schools working in partnership with parents. The discussion focuses on parental involvement with children's education, effective parent–teacher relationships and parent support groups.

Parental involvement with children's education

In recent years government legislation and guidance has extended the parental role in the assessment and decision-making involved when a child has special educational needs. Local authorities are required to provide access to parent partnership services which offer independent advice and support. These services as well as schools work towards enabling parents to:

- recognise and fulfil their full responsibilities as parents and play an active and valued role in their children's education;

- have knowledge of their child's entitlement within the SEN framework;

- make their views known about how their child is educated;

- have access to information, advice and support during assessment and any related decision-making processes about special educational provision.

(DfES, 2001: 2.2.)

If a child is diagnosed with ADHD or displays characteristics associated with the disorder, the above points are particularly important. A cause for concern regarding the learning or behaviour of a student may be raised by parents, teachers or other professionals. It is important that schools work closely with parents who may be unfamiliar with how to obtain additional support for their child or what a diagnosis of ADHD might involve. If medication is used or is being considered as an intervention parents and carers need multi-professional support and advice throughout the assessment process and in monitoring the effectiveness of the medication (see Chapters 2 and 3).

Case study

Adam – school support

Adam had shown cause for concern from the beginning of his school career. Documentary evidence when he was in his first year at primary school confirmed that he showed 'many of the characteristics of ADHD'. Adam's parents were initially against the idea of having him assessed for a possible ADHD diagnosis, mainly because his mother was concerned about the use of medication.

School staff offered as much support as possible, including involving the local Learning Behaviour and Support Service and Speech and Language Therapy Service when Adam was placed on the SEN register under the Code of Practice procedure (DfES, 2001). Despite the school's best efforts, by the time Adam reached 8 years of age it was clear that the gap between him and his peers was widening, both in academic and behavioural areas.

After further discussion with the school, Adam's parents finally agreed to his referral via the school nurse to a community paediatrician for ADHD assessment. Six months later Adam received a formal diagnosis of ADHD and was prescribed Ritalin.

 Case study

Carl's ADHD management

Throughout his time in primary school the SENCO had built up a very good relationship with Carl and his parents. She worked hard on their behalf to obtain extra classroom support and an ADHD diagnosis. Several months after his initial diagnosis of ADHD and prescription of Ritalin, Carl's parents were extremely concerned over a lack of continuity with the local Child and Adolescent Mental Health Service (CAMHS), due in part to the long-term sickness of a consultant child psychiatrist. They were unsure as to what course of action they should take. Following the intervention of the SENCO, a consultant community paediatrician became involved and more regular reviews took place.

Some local authorities or Child and Adolescent Mental Health Services offer parent training in behavioural modification strategies and effective child management techniques for use at home with a child who may be diagnosed with ADHD. It is important that parents are made aware of any interventions or behaviour management techniques being used with the student at school so that they can be reinforced at home. Efforts should be made to ensure that the student receives the same type of support at home and at school.

Teachers can encourage parents to:

- set aside time to work with the child/encourage them to do their homework;

- prepare a quiet time/area that is conducive to the way the child learns in class;

- avoid confrontational situations;

- allow the child a calming down period in times of distress;

- distract the child from dysfunctional behaviour;

- promote their positive characteristics;

- provide structure during holidays so that they know what is expected of them;

- provide boundaries that they understand;

- encourage organisational and timekeeping skills by setting small tasks;

- find ways of promoting their self-esteem;

- encourage outlets for active behaviour.

(Hughes and Cooper, 2007: 89–90)

Parents should also be kept up to date with more general classroom strategies being used at school. Some of the self-esteem enhancement activities mentioned in Chapter 7 can be used at home with parents to reinforce some of the work started at school. 'Many schools have launched their work on the [SEAL] curriculum materials with a specially planned workshop for parents/carers that explores the skills children will be developing' (DfES, 2005: 24).

Student voice

In addition to parental involvement all children and young people should be involved in any decisions that will affect them. Their views on any educational support should be taken into account (DCSF, 2007). This is particularly important in the case of students who may be assessed for a diagnosis of ADHD. The assessment should include in-depth interviews with the child or young person. Parents should ensure that the child is fully involved throughout the identification, diagnosis and decision-making processes regarding interventions, especially those involving medication. At school teachers have a responsibility to ensure that the student is involved in deciding on the most appropriate classroom interventions. Individual Education Plan (IEP) targets should be set following discussions with the student and his or her parents who should be invited to attend any reviews with school and other professionals.

Parent–teacher relationships

The key factor in successful working with parents is the establishing and maintaining of effective parent–teacher or home–school relationships. When dealing with individuals displaying ADHD characteristics there can often be initial difficulties in the parent–teacher relationship, with one party blaming the other for the student's difficulties, especially in cases where a formal assessment of ADHD has not been made. The parents, mothers in particular, may feel that they are being blamed by teachers as well as other parents for their apparent inability to manage their child. Some children with ADHD may behave better with their fathers, causing conflict between the parents, with the father blaming the mother for not keeping the child under control. This can lead to feelings of helplessness and loss of confidence and self-esteem in the mothers and eventually to breakdowns in domestic life. The fact that approximately 40 per cent of parents have or have had symptoms of ADHD may make matters worse in the home situation. Adults who display behaviours such as inattention, hyperactivity and impulsivity as well as difficulties with time management and organisation will find it difficult to support a child who needs uncomplicated daily routines and support with organising themselves and tasks.

At school the teacher may feel that she is being blamed for the behaviour of the student with ADHD and also criticised for not being able to deal with the problem. Teachers have to manage a classroom full of children which may be being totally disrupted by the behaviour of one student. It can be difficult for the teacher to find positive ways of interacting with a child who may be inattentive, hyperactive and impulsive and who does not respond to behavioural management strategies that are effective with other students. The teacher may, albeit subconsciously, attach some blame to the parents for the child's difficulties. When parents and teacher discuss the child's difficulties, it is important to avoid anger, criticism and blame and to be clear that it is no one's fault. 'The importance of establishing and maintaining a positive, co-operative parent–teacher partnership focused on advocacy for the child is paramount' (Cooper and Bilton, 2002: 46).

During the case study research it was reported to the researcher that, in retrospect, Carl's mother believed that she herself had suffered from ADHD symptoms as a girl, but claims to have grown out of it at about 18 years of age. She only realised this when Carl's problems surfaced. No one seemed to have heard of ADHD when she was a girl and she received very little support in school. Parents who had negative experiences in their own education may be reluctant to become involved with their child's school as this may bring back unhappy memories for them. Teachers should develop good communication skills involving active listening and studying body language in order to ensure that meetings with parents go as smoothly as possible. They should make it clear that they value the parents' views and opinions. Teachers come and go over a student's school life but parents are experts on their own child. The amount of time that a student spends in school is approximately 15–18 per cent of an average school year. This means that for at least 80 per cent of the time the child is under the parents' influence (O'Regan, 2005).

Regular contact

There should be continuous two-way communication between teachers and parents. Home–school liaison can take the form of telephone calls, texts or a diary which the student takes from teacher to parent and back again, preferably on a daily basis, to help prevent misunderstandings occurring between home and school. As students with ADHD are prone to forgetfulness, a reminder from the teacher of which day a PE kit or a homework assignment needs to be brought in to school could help prevent difficult situations. The diary should contain details of anything in either setting which may affect the child or young person. For example, if something has happened at home overnight or over the weekend which could have an adverse effect on the student's behaviour the parent should inform the teacher. This could include his not taking medication at home. Two of the boys in the case studies (Edward and Adam) lived with their mothers and their new partners. They each spent some time with their biological father, often a weekend, and this temporary change in living arrangements could cause changes in the students' behaviour. Also some individuals are prescribed Ritalin for school days only, as in Carl's case. He was reported as often being particularly hyperactive on Monday mornings following a weekend at home or after a school holiday.

In addition to any problems which may arise at home or school it is important that parents and teachers make a point of reporting good work and behaviour and that achievements are reinforced in both settings. Of course there is always the possibility of the home–school diary or a note being lost or forgotten, and so whenever possible personal contact between teacher and parent is advisable. A quick word at the school gate at the beginning or end of the day could help prepare teacher or parent for any possible problems or changes in behaviour or provide an opportunity to praise and reward the student.

Adolescents

In a secondary or high school setting regular contact between home and school can be more difficult to maintain than in a pre-school or primary school. Depending on the organisation of the particular school, arrangements could be made for the registration class teacher, head of year or SENCO to liaise with other teachers regarding the student's behaviour and learning on a regular basis. The member of staff who acts as a point of contact within the school can maintain an effective and proactive relationship with parents. Lovey (1999) describes the successful use of small laminated reminder cards (mentioned in Chapter 6) in a high school. Separate cards were made in green, amber and red. Staff were asked to leave a brief note in the SENCO's pigeon hole if there had been any problems with a particular student during the day. The colour of the card sent home depended on how the day had gone. A red card indicated considerable difficulties and the parents were advised to contact the school as soon as possible. An amber card meant that the difficulties should be discussed by the parents with the student. A green card signifying good work or behaviour provided an opportunity to reinforce school achievements at home. Parents of adolescents should also be encouraged to become involved in the completion of the student's homework book. Effective liaison between home and school may lead to the amount of homework being reduced and there should be acknowledgement of the effort that goes into completing homework assignments (Kewley, 1999).

Parent support groups and other voluntary agencies

Parent support groups have an important role to play in offering advice and support for families and in providing information on ADHD and referral procedures. It is helpful for parents and carers to be able to meet with other parents who know the kind of challenges and problems they may have to face in living with children with ADHD. Clinicians, schools or local authorities should be able to provide details of local groups. Some of the many websites providing details of national and local groups are included in the list of useful organisations and websites at the end of this book.

National groups work on raising awareness of ADHD, holding conferences and meetings which are attended by professionals and parents. The rise in numbers of parent support groups is an indication of the way in which labels such as ADHD are no longer associated with stigma. Instead they are viewed as a source of empowerment and as a means of securing additional funding and resources. A recent conference organised by the national parent support group ADDISS (Attention Deficit Disorder Information and Support Service) was attended by 400 parents and resulted in the production of a report about parents' experiences. More than half of the parents reported that a support group had been the most valuable resource for them (ADDISS, 2003). The two ADHD study days arranged by the researcher (reported in Chapter 5) included parents among the delegates. On each occasion a presentation offering a parent's perspective from a member of a local ADHD support group was included in the multi-professional programme.

This chapter has moved outside the school setting and begun the focus on the wider context by highlighting the importance of parental involvement and home–school relationships. The final chapter will go further by drawing conclusions and making recommendations for how future policy and practice might contribute to more effective working with ADHD.

 Points to remember

- The wider environment can affect what goes on in school.
- Parents can play an important role in the education of their children.
- The views of the student should be taken into account.
- There should be continuous two-way communication between teachers and parents.
- Approximately 40 per cent of parents have or have had symptoms of ADHD.
- Parent support groups provide a significant role in supporting families of children with ADHD.

 Questions for reflection and discussion

1. What information from parents and carers would be useful in teaching students with ADHD?
2. What information can schools provide to parents and carers that would help in the management of the disorder at home?
3. What steps can be taken to ensure that students' views on educational interventions are taken into account?

9

Conclusions and recommendations

> The final chapter discusses the points raised in previous chapters, focusing on several key issues involved in effective inclusive education for students with ADHD. These centre on:
>
> - increased and effective training for all educational practitioners, leading to increased pedagogical and curricular flexibility in schools; and
> - multi-professional approaches to identification and management of ADHD.
>
> Recommendations for the future for the effective management of ADHD include:
>
> - acknowledgement of the concept of ADHD in future national guidance;
> - increased awareness, knowledge and expertise;
> - more school-based research into ADHD;
> - an increase in investment in training for all educational practitioners;
> - improvements in multi-professional involvements in ADHD; and
> - more research into medication effects.

> The educational environment operates at four levels: national and local educational policy, the school itself, the classroom and the teacher's approach to the individual child. For best results, strategies at all four levels must reflect an awareness of the needs and difficulties of the child with ADHD. (Kewley, 1999: 145)

The chapters in Section 2 have examined the last three levels. This final chapter will continue the discussion of the wider context by drawing on points raised in the previous chapters to focus on several key issues involved in effective inclusive education for students with ADHD and highlighting the implications of the research findings for future policy and practice.

The reality of ADHD

Controversy exists around ADHD on several levels, including the general abstract concept of the disorder, its manifestations in everyday life and assessment procedures, but the evolving concept of ADHD cannot be ignored. The different terminology used over the years indicates the changes in perceptions of the nature of the disorder. As mentioned in Chapter 1 there have been published references to characteristics associated with the disorder from possibly as far back as the nineteenth century. The term

'ADHD' has been in use since 1987. 'In our lifetime it is likely that the diagnostic label will change again. There are many who argue for example that we should call this condition Behavioural Inhibition Disorder (BID) ...' (Holowenko, 1999: 14).

ADHD is one of the most widely studied childhood disorders and there continues to be debate over the core symptoms, diagnosis, causes, prevalence, prognosis and the effects of interventions, in particular medication. The most fundamental debate has centred on the reality or the very existence of such a disorder. In the US, Professor Russell Barkley took the unprecedented step of issuing an 'International Consensus Statement on ADHD' in which he and 74 prominent medical doctors and researchers confirmed the status of the scientific findings concerning the validity of the disorder (Barkley et al., 2002). This immediately stimulated additional debate and led to Timimi and 33 co-endorsers publishing a 'Critique of the International Consensus Statement on ADHD' (Timimi et al., 2004). The debate goes on. Even those who do not acknowledge the existence of ADHD, as diagnosed using DSM-IV criteria (APA, 2000), can be in no doubt that there are students who display some or all of the features of inattention, hyperactivity, impulsivity and associated difficulties in classroom settings. In order to provide effective inclusive education, it is necessary for those students to be identified early on so that they can receive the appropriate support to enable them to access the curriculum and to achieve their full potential.

There is generally no specific mention of ADHD in government publications. Guidance for schools on data collection by type of SEN suggests that students diagnosed with ADHD should be included in the category Behavioural, Emotional and Social Difficulty (BESD) if additional or different educational arrangements are being made to support them. The term BESD covers a wide range of SEN. It is particularly important that ADHD is acknowledged by government departments as a discrete disorder which requires specific support appropriate to the needs of those individuals with a diagnosis.

Prevalence

In the school survey the prevalence rate for ADHD in a local authority was found to be approximately 0.5 per cent (5 students per 1,000), with the rate in the population of the schools involved in the case study research approximately 0.6 per cent. These rates may be conservative estimates of actual prevalence, with suggestions that the disorder is underdiagnosed. If schools' own estimates are taken into consideration, prevalence rates would be nearer the 1 per cent of the total school population suggested in published figures (NICE, 2000). The survey findings also indicate a boy:girl ratio of 9:1. It is important to take into account the different ADHD subtypes. Cooper and Bilton suggest 'girls and women are just as likely to have ADD/ without hyperactivity as are boys and men [and that] girls with ADHD face similar difficulties, yet often without gaining the attention of parents and teachers' (2002: 87). There is a need for increasing the awareness and knowledge of all subtypes of ADHD among professionals involved in the identification and diagnosis of the disorder.

A prevalence rate of 0.5–1 per cent of the total school population with a diagnosis of ADHD has implications for future planning for the successful inclusion of students in mainstream education. The highest rates were reported among students in the 7–11 years age group in the school survey. When funding issues are addressed it is important that primary schools in particular have access to sufficient resources to aid them in supporting students with ADHD.

Variability in ADHD symptoms and associated difficulties

Educational practitioners working in mainstream schools and early years settings are now extremely likely to come into contact with students displaying ADHD symptoms. There are wide-ranging differences in ADHD characteristics displayed by students across settings and over time. There are also variations in the number and severity of comorbid and associated features experienced by individual students with ADHD. No two individuals with ADHD are the same. It is for this reason that all teachers need to develop an understanding of the theoretical nature of the disorder so that they can develop approaches and practical strategies for use with students in the classroom. There is still a great deal to be learned about how best to enhance the performance of students who display characteristics associated with ADHD. In order to explore and understand more about ADHD in school settings, there is a need for further school-based research to be undertaken into situational and temporal variability of ADHD symptoms (Wheeler et al., 2009).

The need for pedagogical and curricular flexibility

The case study research has found that students with ADHD generally display approximately 30 per cent more ADHD (or off-task) behaviours than their non-ADHD classmates and that this figure is stable over time. It is interesting to note that during the observations in the case studies it was found that even the non-ADHD students displayed some ADHD behaviours in some settings (on average, target students displayed 45 per cent and comparison students 14 per cent ADHD behaviours). This could be interpreted as a reflection on the current delivery of the curriculum and could suggest that the educational environment partly causes or exacerbates these behaviours (Cooper, 2005). The following examples are taken from case studies provided in earlier chapters which reported selected ITS observation findings:

- Although both Carl and Ian were focused on the video at the beginning of the history lesson reported in Chapter 5 (Figure 5.2), neither concentrated as well during the less structured class brainstorming session or the written task towards the end of the afternoon.

- In the DT lesson (Figure 5.5) both David and John concentrated throughout most of the practical part of the lesson which involved the use of a kinaesthetic learning approach. Both displayed more ADHD behaviours during the introductory carpet session and even more during the final carpet session at the end of a long afternoon lesson.

- During the science lesson on a wet day, described in Chapter 4 (Figure 4.11), Carl's ADHD behaviours were higher than normal in science lessons and also higher in all other lessons for that day. Ian also displayed slightly more ADHD behaviours that day when there was no opportunity for the class to go outside for physical exercise at playtimes.

Changes to conceptualisations of the curriculum are needed. The delivery and organisation of lessons should reflect the positive aspects of ADHD characteristics. There should be a variety of teaching and learning approaches, increased flexibility in grouping and support in the classroom, a combination of proactive and reactive strategies and further use of nurture group settings where appropriate. If possible, periods of structured physical activity should be included throughout the school day. More effective approaches and interventions in school might mean fewer students needing medication.

At the time of writing, students in their final year of primary school in England are required to take SATs in core subjects, the results of which are published and used for school accountability purposes. There is much debate regarding the continuation of SAT testing and the publication of school league tables. Schools are often accused of carrying out extensive test preparation and practice sessions. The UK government stresses the importance of SATs at the age of 11 years to provide a measure of achievement at the transition from primary to secondary school. An over-reliance on testing does not help students with ADHD and associated cognitive difficulties. More use of teacher assessment and an increased emphasis on vocational qualifications might assist these students. There are calls for PSHE to be included as part of the statutory National Curriculum and programmes such as SEAL have been recommended for use in early years and school settings. Individuals with ADHD who experience associated affective difficulties would benefit from these proposals. Any future curricular reforms should take into account the above suggestions.

Increased and effective training for all educational practitioners

It is essential for all educational practitioners to be provided with opportunities to increase their knowledge and expertise in supporting students who display ADHD characteristics in the school situation. In addition to the suggestions above focusing on increased flexibility in the curriculum teachers also need to be aware of how some of the more conventional classroom and behaviour management strategies can be used to deal with specific ADHD behaviours, as highlighted in Chapter 6. The concluding section of Chapter 6 also emphasises the importance of whole-school approaches and policies for ADHD. It is important that all school staff, teaching and non-teaching, who may come into contact with students with ADHD, have an understanding of the nature of the disorder and its implications.

Chapter 5 refers to findings from the research and two ADHD study days indicating that relevant training and support for educational practitioners has not so far generally been available. According to a recent report in the *Times Educational Supplement*, of the 10 out of 85 teacher training institutions in England and Wales who replied to a question on training in ADHD, 'Six hours' training during a three-year course was the most offered. Three colleges offered nothing, one said two hours and the others an hour or less. Two admitted they offered ten minutes' (Stewart, 2006: 23). There is a need for increased investment in training for teachers at both the initial training stage and as part of in-service training and continuing professional development. Support staff should also receive relevant training and be provided with access to research, seminars and information. In order that SENCOs, teachers and support staff may work together effectively in supporting students with ADHD and associated difficulties, training in the management and deployment of TAs is also needed. All courses, including shorter postgraduate teacher training courses such as the PGCE (Postgraduate Certificate in Education), should ensure that new teachers are fully prepared to teach students with a range of SEN including ADHD.

Special schools

The focus of this book has been on the inclusion of students with ADHD in mainstream settings. Occasionally a student may experience such severe difficulties due to ADHD and possibly other coexisting difficulties that a mainstream setting is inappropriate. Some may need to be educated on a full- or part-time basis in pupil referral units or in special schools which may focus specifically on students with EBD or severe or moderate learning difficulties. The requirements of national guidance on SEN may be interpreted differently by different local authorities. It is important that parental views are taken into account and that each individual student is placed in the setting which is best suited to meeting his or her needs.

Some special schools in the UK closed as a result of the inclusion agenda but recently it has been recognised that they have an important contribution to make in sharing their expertise and working with mainstream schools to provide extra support strategies for use with students with disorders such as ADHD. Increased collaboration, greater staff movement and more students moving between sectors has been encouraged (DfES, 2004). It is important that this collaboration continues.

Improvements in multi-professional involvements in ADHD

Government guidance recognises 'the need to bring specialist services together, working in multi-disciplinary teams, to focus on the needs of the child' (DfES, 2004: 25). Unfortunately, such advice advocating a collaborative approach is often vague about the reality of how this might happen. As highlighted in Chapter 3 there can be variability in multi-professional and multi-agency involvements in ADHD. Changes in attitudes to diagnostic classifications and labels such as ADHD could help improve the support available to individual students. It is important that steps are taken to ensure closer working between professionals, parents and students. There is a particular need for improvements in access to CAMHS and more effective communication between health professionals, parents and young people at the time of transition from child to adult health services.

There is a need for raised awareness of pathways for referral and care and also training in ADHD for all professionals involved in the identification and management of the disorder as well as parents and carers. In the UK specialist staff in some local authorities and some health services may offer relevant training and information. Some training providers now offer postgraduate courses in Integrated Children's Services which focus on the analysis and development of collaborative strategies and effective provision of children's services. The development of integrated or multi-agency services could help overcome operational difficulties in multi-professional working.

Medication

Effective multi-professional collaboration is particularly important when medication is used as part of a multi-modal intervention and there is a need for effects to be closely monitored in home and school settings. Previous chapters have included references to the controversy surrounding the use of medication as an intervention for ADHD. Reported benefits include improvements in classroom behaviour, attention and concentration and in peer and family relationships. Positive changes in behaviour and concentration were reported in 70 per cent of cases in the school survey. In the majority of cases, any side effects can be controlled by adjusting the dosage.

New types and formulations of drugs have been developed over the years, with stimulant and non-stimulant, short-acting and sustained release versions of drugs now available. In the US, methylphenidate skin patches have recently been licensed for the treatment of 6–12 year olds with ADHD. A patch is attached to the child's hip and is effective for nine hours, although it may continue to be effective for another three hours after removal (Anderson and Scott, 2006). This type of treatment could be beneficial in cases where a child or young person has difficulty in swallowing tablets, does not respond to other treatments or experiences more severe side effects. There has been research focusing on an examination of medication as an intervention, but there is still a need for further research into (a) the long-term effects of different types of medication, (b) different formulations of medication and (c) students' perceptions of the positive and negative effects of medication.

Recommendations

The key issues discussed in this chapter centre on two major themes: variability in ADHD symptoms leading to the need for increased pedagogical and curricular flexibility in schools; and improvements in multi-professional approaches to the identification, assessment and management of ADHD. The majority of recommendations summarised below are concerned with raising awareness of the concept of ADHD and the need for further research into various aspects of the disorder.

Summary of recommendations

- Acknowledgement of ADHD in national guidance.

- A raising of awareness of all ADHD subtypes among professionals.

- Sufficient resources for all schools to support students with ADHD.

- More school-based research into variability of ADHD symptoms.

- Increased pedagogical and curricular flexibility.

- Whole-school policies on ADHD.

- Increased investment in training for educational practitioners.

- Improvements in multi-professional involvements in ADHD, with more integrated services.

- More research into medication – long-term efficacy, new formulations and student perceptions of the effects.

 Questions for reflection and discussion

1. Has this book succeeded in answering your initial questions on the concept of ADHD?
2. What are the most important things you have learned?
3. What do you believe are the most pressing concerns about provision for the education of students with ADHD?

Appendix A

Section 1: Background to ADHD

The ADHD Toolkit

SECTION 1
Background to the concept of ADHD

1

What is ADHD?

A medical disorder diagnosed by a clinician (paediatrician or child psychiatrist)

Three core symptoms:

- Inattentiveness
- Hyperactivity
- Impulsivity

2

To be considered for ADHD assessment:

- Individual displays 6 or more symptoms of inattention and/or 6 or more symptoms of hyperactivity–impulsivity
- Some of the 3 main symptoms present before age 7
- Symptoms present for at least 6 months
- Symptoms occur in more than one setting (e.g. home and school)
- Evidence of significant impairment in social and academic functioning
- Symptoms not accounted for by any other mental disorder

3

The concept of ADHD

- Diagnosis – differences in approaches
- History – changes to terminology
- Causes – multi-factorial
- Prevalence – variations
- Coexisting problems – social, emotional, educational
- Prognosis – long-term outcome
- Interventions – medical, educational and social

4

Use of medication

- Types and use of medication
- Numbers of pupils taking medication
- Reported effectiveness
- Differing viewpoints

5

Multi-professional involvements

- A multi-professional approach in assessment and management of ADHD
- Parental and school involvements in identification and monitoring procedures
- Differences in attitudes and awareness

6

 The ADHD Toolkit © Linda Wheeler, 2010 (SAGE)

Appendix B

Section 2: The School Setting

The ADHD Toolkit

SECTION 2

The school setting

1

Systematic classroom observation
(1) Fixed interval sampling (FIS)

- Target student only is observed
- Recordings are made of predominant behaviour at 15-second intervals
- Provides data on frequency and duration of behaviour
- Can be used in any setting for lessons of varying lengths

2

FIS data analysis

Carl, aged 10 years		No ADHD	ADHD behaviours	
Date	Context		Inatt'n	Hyp–Imp
Thur 4 Dec 13:54 – 35 minutes	**Design & Technology lesson** Half class (N = 12) working outside main classroom with teacher Modifying model chassis, adding motor	88%	9%	3%
Fri 15 Nov 10:20 – 28 minutes	**Assembly** Whole school in hall (N = 440 students, HT, teachers, TAs) 'Children in Need' day	28%	34%	38%

3

FIS data analysis

Carl, aged 9 years		No ADHD	ADHD behaviours	
Date	Context		Inatt'n	Hyp–Imp
Wed 25 Sep 11:00 – 60 minutes	**Literacy lesson** – group (N = 4) Working with TA, SENCO Six short, varied activities (very little writing involved)	88%	7%	5%
Mon 30 Sep 09:17 – 50 minutes	**Numeracy lesson** – group (N = 4) Working with TA) Number bonds to 10; addition and subtraction games	35%	21%	44%

4

Systematic classroom observation
(2) Instantaneous time sampling (ITS)

- Target student and non-ADHD comparison are observed
- 'Snapshot' of behaviour recorded at 30-second intervals
- Used over a ten-minute period (20 observations), or three periods in different parts of a lesson

5

ITS data analysis

Date, time at which 10-minute recording period began	Context, part of lesson	Carl (Target student)			Ian (Comparison)		
		No AD/HD	Inatt	H/I	No AD/HD	Inatt	H/I
Mon 15 Sep 13:36	**History** – 2 classes of 10 yr olds Start – watch video	16	1	3	20	0	0
13:57	Middle – class discussion	3	8	9	11	6	3
14:28	End – writing, worksheet	5	12	3	13	7	0
Mon 25 Nov	**Art** –group (N = 5) in art area outside classroom						
14:00	Start – apply hot wax to Batik	18	1	1	19	1	0
14:24	Middle – draw design on material	17	3	0	16	4	0
14:44	End – Reapply hot wax	18	2	0	19	1	0

6

(Continued)

(Continued)

ITS data analysis

Date, time at which 10-minute recording period began	Context, part of lesson	Carl (Target student)			Ian (Comparison)		
		No AD/HD	ADHD Inatt	H/I	No AD/HD	ADHD Inatt	H/I
Thu 20 Nov	**Science** – class 10 – 11 yr olds, group						
11:30	Start – Write up experiment 1	5	12	3	13	6	1
11:50	Middle – T introduces experiment 2	16	4	0	18	2	0
12:02	End – Experiment 2 – separating solids	20	0	0	20	0	0
Tues 15 Oct	**Science** – class 9 –10 yr olds						
14:03	Start – Devise tables 'Changes'	6	5	9	16	3	1
14:27	Middle – Class discussion, ideas	6	7	7	15	3	2
14:40	End – Draw cross section of fruit	5	9	6	14	4	2

7

General classroom strategies

Refer to checklists in Chapter 6 for:

- Inattention:
  - Classroom layout
  - Sustaining attention
  - Time management and organisation
- Hyperactivity
- Impulsiveness

8

Behaviour management strategies

- Rules – consistent, positive, clearly displayed
- Involve pupils in deciding rewards and sanctions
- Remain calm, do not shout
- Model appropriate behaviour at all times
- Rewards – value good behaviour with rewards
- Reprimands – short and given at time of incident
- Interventions – time-out, ignore-rules-praise, token economies, behavioural contracts
- Positive behaviour-related comments to be made 4 times as often as negative comments

9

Associated difficulties

- Cognitive diffculties
- Affective diffculties
  - Emotional immaturity
  - Social relationships
  - Self-esteem
- Other difficulties

10

Appendix C
Section 3: The Wider Context

The ADHD Toolkit

SECTION 3

The wider context

1

Working with parents

- Parental involvement with child's education
- Effective parent–teacher relationships
- Parent support groups
- See also: 'ADHD information for parents' PowerPoint presentation

2

Conclusions

Key issues:
- The reality of ADHD
- Prevalence and possible under-diagnosis of the disorder
- Variability in ADHD symptoms and associated difficulties
- Pedagogical and curricular flexibility
- Increased and effective training for all educational practitioners
- Improvements in multi-professional involvements in ADHD
- The use of medication

3

Recommendations

- Acknowledgement of ADHD in national guidance
- A raising of awareness of all ADHD subtypes among professionals
- Sufficient resources for all schools to support students with ADHD
- More school-based research into variability of ADHD symptoms
- Increased pedagogical and curricular flexibility
- Whole-school policies on ADHD
- Increased investment in training for educational practitioners
- Improvements in multi-professional involvements in ADHD, with more integrated services
- More research into medication

4

 The ADHD Toolkit © Linda Wheeler, 2010 (SAGE)

Appendix D
ADHD information for parents

The ADHD Toolkit

ADHD informaton for parents

1

What is ADHD?

A medical disorder diagnosed by a clinician (paediatrician or child psychiatrist)

Three core symptoms:

- Inattention
- Hyperactivity
- Impulsivity

2

Inattention

- Fails to give close attention to details
- Difficulty sustaining attention
- Does not appear to listen
- Difficulty following through instructions
- Avoids tasks requiring sustained mental effort
- Difficulty in organising tasks and activities
- Loses things necessary for tasks and activities
- Easily distracted by extraneous stimuli
- Being forgetful in daily activities

3

Hyperactivity

- Fidgets with hands or feet
- Unauthorised movement in the classroom
- Runs about or climbs excessively in situations where it is inappropriate
- Has difficulty in playing quietly
- Is often 'on the go'
- Talks excessively

4

Impulsivity

- Blurts out answers

- Difficulty awaiting turn

- Interrupts or intrudes upon others (butts in)

5

To be considered for ADHD assessment:

- Individual displays 6 or more symptoms of inattention and/or 6 or more symptoms of hyperactivity–impulsivity
- Some of the 3 main symptoms present before age 7
- Symptoms present for at least 6 months
- Symptoms occur in more than one setting (e.g. home and school)
- Evidence of significant impairment in social and academic functioning
- Symptoms not accounted for by any other mental disorder

6

(Continued)

(Continued)

Other difficulties associated with ADHD

- Learning difficulties
- Speech and language development
- Disruptive behaviour disorders
- Emotional immaturity
- Social skills problems
- Poor self-esteem
- Poor motor control – difficulties with handwriting and dressing
- Oversensitivity

7

What can be done in school (1)

- Flexibility in delivery and organisation of the curriculum
- Awareness of differing teaching and learning styles
- Variation in grouping and support in the classroom

8

What can be done in school (2)

- Classroom management strategies including:
  - attention to classroom layout, including seating
  - help with sustaining attention
  - help with time management and organisation
- Behaviour management strategies
- Social skills training
- Enhancing self esteem
- Whole-school policies and support

9

What can done at home

- Set aside time to work with the child/ encourage them to do their homework
- Prepare a quiet time/area for the child
- Avoid confrontational situations
- Allow the child a calming down period in times of distress
- Distract the child from unwanted behaviour
- Promote their positive characteristics
- Provide structure during holidays
- Provide boundaries that they understand
- Encourage organisational and time-keeping skills by setting small tasks
- Find ways of promoting their self-esteem
- Encourage outlets for active behaviour

10

Importance of good home–school relationships

- Early cause for concern can come from parent or teacher
- Completed questionnaires required from home and school as part of ADHD assessment
- Regular two-way communication is essential
- Monitoring of medication effects at home and school
- Views of student should be taken into account

11

Appendix E

Instantaneous Time Sampling Observation Analysis

Date, time at which 10-minute recording period began, part of lesson	Lesson	Recordings out of 20					
		Target student			Comparison student		
		0	ADHD behaviours		0	ADHD behaviours	
			Inatt	H/I		Inatt	H/I

 The ADHD Toolkit © Linda Wheeler, 2010 (SAGE)

Appendix F

Fixed Interval Sampling Observation analysis

Date, time, duration	Context	No ADHD	ADHD behaviours	
			Inattention	Hyperactivity/ Impulsivity

 The ADHD Toolkit © Linda Wheeler, 2010 (SAGE)

Glossary and abbreviations

ABC	Antecedents, behaviour and consequences approach
ADD	Attention deficit disorder
ADDISS	Attention Deficit Disorder Information and Support Service
ADHD	Attention deficit hyperactivity disorder
Amphetamine	Type of stimulant drug
APA	American Psychiatric Association
ASD	Autistic spectrum disorders
Atomoxetine	A non-stimulant drug (Strattera)
BESD	Behavioural, Emotional and Social Difficulty
BID	Behavioural inhibition disorder
Bio-psycho-social	Influenced by biological, psychological and social factors
BPS	British Psychological Society
CAMHS	Child and Adolescent Mental Health Services
CD	Conduct disorder
Concerta	Once-daily sustained release version of methylphenidate
DAMP	Deficits in Attention, Motor Control and Perception
DCD	Development coordination disorder
DCSF	Department for Children, Schools and Families
Dexamphetamine	Type of stimulant drug (for example, Dexedrine, Adderall)
DfES	Department for Education and Skills
DLA	Disability Living Allowance
Dopamine	A neurotransmitter; a chemical compound occurring in the brain that aids selective attention
DSM-IV (TR)	*Diagnostic and Statistical Manual of Mental Disorders* (4th edn) text revision (APA, 2000)

DT	Design and Technology
Dyscalculia	A condition associated with specific learning difficulties in mathematics
EBD	Emotional and behavioural difficulties
FIS	Fixed interval sampling – systematic observation in which behaviour is recorded over fixed intervals of time
Hyperactivity	Excessive levels of activity
HKD	Hyperkinetic disorder – persistent impaired attention and hyperactivity
ICD-10	*International Classification of Diseases* (10th edn) (WHO, 1990)
ICT	Information and communication technology
Impulsivity, impulsiveness	Suddenly saying or doing things without thinking, having little sense of danger
Inattention	Difficulty in concentrating, paying attention
IEP	Individual Education Plan – a document which sets out what a student needs to achieve and how he will be helped to do so
INSET	In-service education and training
ITS	Instantaneous time sampling – systematic observation in which behaviour is recorded at pre-determined moments in time
LBSS	Learning and Behaviour Support Service
Methylphenidate	Stimulant drug (Ritalin is the most common form)
Neurotransmitter	A chemical messenger in the brain that carries information between nerve cells
NHS	National Health Service
NICE	National Institute for Health and Clinical Excellence
Noradrenaline	A neurotransmitter that prompts 'fight or flight' reactions (also known as norepinephrine)
OCD	Obsessive compulsive disorder
ODD	Oppositional defiant disorder
PE	Physical Education
PGCE	Postgraduate Certificate in Education

PRU	Pupil referral unit
PSHE	Personal, Social and Health Education
SAT	Standard Assessment Task
SEAL	Social and Emotional Aspects of Learning
SEN	Special Educational Needs
SENCO	Special Educational Needs Coordinator
SIGN	Scottish Intercollegiate Guidelines Network
SSA	Special support assistant
Statement	A document produced by the local authority outlining a student's needs and the support and additional provision necessary to meet those needs (known as a Record of Need in Scotland)
TA	Teaching assistant
TCA	Tricyclic antidepressant medication
TOAD	Talking out, Out of seat, Attention problems and Disruption
WHO	World Health Organisation

Suggestions for further reading

The following suggestions for further reading are in addition to the sources included in the References section.

Parents

Hoopmann, K. (2008) *All Dogs Have ADHD*. London: Jessica Kingsley.

Munden, A. and Arcelus, J. (1999) *The AD/HD Handbook: A Guide for Parents and Professionals on Attention Deficit/Hyperactivity Disorder*. London: Jessica Kingsley.

National Institute for Health and Clinical Excellence (NICE) (2008) *Understanding NICE Guidance*. London: NICE.

Pentecost, D. (2000) *Parenting the ADD Child: Can't Do? Won't Do?* London: Jessica Kingsley.

Books for children and adolescents

Grindley, S. (2006) *Hurricane Wills*. London: Bloomsbury Publishing (also available as an audio book).

Hensby, C. and Braham, B. (1998) *Hunter of the Past* (downloaded from www.adders.org).

Leigh, J. (2005) *Zak has ADHD: A Doctor Spot Book*. London: Red Kite.

Pigache, P. (2008) *Need to Know ADHD*. Oxford: Heinemann Library.

Spilsbury, L. (2001) *What Does It Mean to Have Attention Deficit Hyperactivity Disorder?* Oxford: Heinemann Library.

Self-esteem

Collins, M. and Drakeford, P. (2002) *Because I'm Special: A Take-home Programme to Enhance Self-Esteem in Children Aged 6–9*. Bristol: Lucky Duck Publishing.

Lawrence, D. (1996) *Enhancing Self-Esteem in the Classroom*, 2nd edn. London: Paul Chapman Publishing.

Plummer, D. (2007) *Helping Children to Build Self-Esteem: A Photocopiable Activities Book*, 2nd edn. London: Jessica Kingsley.

Alternative/complementary interventions

Jacobs, J., Williams, A., Girard, C., Njike, V. Y. and Katz, D. (2005) 'Homeopathy for attention deficit/hyperactivity disorder: a pilot randomised controlled trial', *Journal of Alternative and Complementary Medicine,* 11 (5): 799–806.

Jensen, P. S. and Kenny, D. T. (2004) 'The effects of yoga on the attention and behaviour of boys with attention deficit/hyperactivity disorder', *Journal of Attention Disorders*, 7 (4): 205–16.

Kinder, J. (1999a) 'ADHD – a different viewpoint I: dietary factors', in P. Cooper and K. Bilton (eds), *Attention Deficit Hyperactivity Disorder (ADHD): Research, Practice and Opinion.* London: Whurr Publishers, pp. 76–110.

Kinder, J. (1999b) 'ADHD – a different viewpoint II: holistic and other approaches', in P. Cooper and K. Bilton (eds), *Attention Deficit Hyperactivity Disorder (ADHD): Research, Practice and Opinion.* London: Whurr Publishers, pp. 111–37.

Sinha, D. and Efron, D. (2005) 'Complementary and alternative medicine use in children with attention deficit hyperactivity disorder', *Journal of Paediatrics and Child Health*, 41 (1–2): 23–6.

List of useful organisations and websites

www.adders.org	An ADD/ADHD non-profit-making support group based in Thanet, Kent, UK
www.addiss.co.uk	National Attention Deficit Disorder Information and Support Service (UK)
www.behaviour4learning.ac.uk	Website supported by the Training and Development Agency, includes research in behaviour management
www.nasen.org.uk	UK organisation for special educational needs
www.ni.add.org/uk	Northern Ireland ADHD Support Centre
www.SEBDA.org	Multi-professional social, emotional and behavioural difficulties association
www.sign.ac.uk	Scottish Intercollegiate Guidelines Network
www.sqa.org.uk	Scottish Qualifications Authority
www.teachernet.gov.uk	Developed by the Department for Children, Schools and Families (UK) as a resource to support the education profession
www.teachers.tv	Provides education programmes on TV and online, resources and support materials
www.tda.gov.uk	Training and Development Agency for schools
www.youngminds.org.uk	UK charity which promotes child and adolescent mental health services

References

ADDISS (2003) *ADHD: Parents, Provision and Policy: A Consultation with Parents*. London: ADDISS.

Alban-Metcalfe, J. and Alban-Metcalfe, J. (2001) *Managing Attention Deficit/Hyperactivity Disorder in the Inclusive Classroom: Practical Strategies for Teachers*. London: David Fulton.

American Psychiatric Association (APA) (2000) *Diagnostic and Statistical Manual of Mental Disorders*, 4th edn, text revision. Washington, DC: APA.

Anderson, V. R. and Scott, L. J. (2006) 'Methylphenidate transdermal system: in attention deficit hyperactivity disorder in children', *Drugs*, 66 (8): 1117–26.

Antshel, K. M. (2005) 'Social skills training reconsidered: what role should peers play?', *The ADHD Report*, 13 (1): 1–5.

Ayers, H., Clarke, D. and Ross, A. (Support for Learning Service, London Borough of Tower Hamlets Children's Service) (1996) *Assessing Individual Needs: A Practical Approach*, 2nd edn. London: David Fulton.

Barkley, R. A. (2006) *Attention-Deficit Hyperactivity Disorder: A Handbook for Diagnosis and Treatment*, 3rd edn. New York: Guilford Press.

Barkley, R. A. and 74 co-endorsers (2002) 'International Consensus Statement on ADHD', *European Child and Adolescent Psychiatry*, 11 (2): 96–8.

Bennathan, M. and Boxall, M. (2000) *Effective Intervention in Primary Schools: Nurture Groups*, 2nd edn. London: David Fulton.

Brettingham, M. (2007) 'Pupils' little helper at 50p a fix', *Times Educational Supplement*, 8 June.

British Psychological Society (BPS) (1996) *Attention Deficit Hyperactivity Disorder: A Psychological Response to an Evolving Concept*. Leicester: British Psychological Society.

British Psychological Society (BPS) (2000) *Attention Deficit Hyperactivity Disorder (ADHD): Guidelines and Principles for Successful Multi-agency Working*. Leicester: British Psychological Society.

CAMHS (2008) *Children and Young People in Mind: The Final Report of the National CAMHS Review*. Downloaded from www.dcsf.gov.uk/CAMHSreview.

Chamberlain, S. and Sahakian, B. (2006) 'Attention Deficit Hyperactivity Disorder has serious and immediate implications', *Educational Journal*, 94 (4): 35–7.

Coghill, D. (2005) 'Attention deficit hyperactivity disorder: should we believe the mass media or peer-reviewed literature?', *Psychiatric Bulletin*, 29: 288–91.

Connelly, G., Lockhart, E., Wilson, P., Furnivall, J., Bryce, G., Harbour, R. and Phin, L. (2008) 'Teachers' responses to the emotional needs of children and young people. Results from the Scottish Needs Assessment Programme', *Emotional and Behavioural Difficulties*, 13 (1): 8–19.

Cooper, P. (2004) *Nurturing Pupils with ADHD*. Paper presented at the 5th World Congress on Dyslexia, Thessaloniki, Greece, August.

Cooper, P. (2005) 'AD/HD', in A. Lewis and B. Norwich (eds), *Special Teaching for Special Children? Pedagogies for Inclusion*. Maidenhead: Open University Press, pp. 123–37.

Cooper, P. (2006) 'Assessing the social and educational value of AD/HD', in M. Hunter-Carsh, Y. Tiknaz, P. Cooper and R. Sage (eds), *The Handbook of Social, Emotional and Behavioural Difficulties*. London: Continuum, pp. 248–63.

Cooper, P. and Bilton, K. (2002) *Attention Deficit/Hyperactivity Disorder: A Practical Guide for Teachers*, 2nd edn. London: David Fulton.

Cooper, P. and O'Regan, F. J. (2001) *Educating Children with AD/HD: A Teacher's Manual*. Abingdon: RoutledgeFalmer.

Cooper, P. and Shea, T. (1999) 'ADHD from the inside: an empirical study of young people's perceptions of the experience of ADHD', in P. Cooper and K. Bilton (eds), *Attention Deficit Hyperactivity Disorder (ADHD): Research, Practice and Opinion*. London: Whurr Publishers, pp. 223–45.

Daniel, S. and Cooper, P. (1999) 'Teachers' classroom strategies for dealing with students with ADHD: an empirical study', in P. Cooper and K. Bilton (eds), *ADHD: Research, Practice and Opinion*. London: Whurr Publishers, pp. 203–22.

Department for Children, Schools and Families (2007) *The Children's Plan*. London: DCSF.

Department for Children, Schools and Families (2008) *Promoting Achievement, Valuing Success: A Strategy for 14–19 Qualifications*. London: DCSF.

Department for Education and Skills (2001) *Special Educational Needs Code of Practice*. London: DfES.

Department for Education and Skills (2003) *Every Child Matters*. London: DfES.

Department for Education and Skills (2004) *Removing Barriers to Achievement: The Government's Strategy for SEN*. London: DfES.

Department for Education and Skills (2005) *Primary National Strategy. Excellence and Enjoyment: Social and Emotional Aspects of Learning*. London: DfES.

Department of Education (2005) *Guidance for Schools: Recording Children with Special Educational Needs*. Downloaded from www.deni.gov.uk.

DuPaul, G. J. and Stoner, G. (1994) *ADHD in the Schools: Assessment and Intervention Strategies*. New York: Guilford Press.

DuPaul, G. J. and Stoner, G. (2003) *ADHD in the Schools: Assessment and Intervention Strategies*, 2nd edn. London: Guilford Press.

DuPaul, G. J. and Weyandt, L. L. (2006) 'School-based interventions for children and adolescents with attention-deficit hyperactivity disorder: enhancing academic and behavioural outcomes', *Education and Treatment of Children*, 29 (2): 341–58.

Gillberg, C. (2002) *The Comorbidities of ADHD: An Underrated Problem*. Paper presented at the Fifth International ADDISS Conference, London, November.

Goldstein, S. (2006) 'Is ADHD a growth industry?', *Journal of Attention Disorders*, 9 (3): 461–4.

Goldstein, S. and Goldstein, M. (1998) *Managing Attention Deficit Hyperactivity Disorder in Children*, 2nd edn. New York: John Wiley & Sons.

Green, C. and Chee, K. (1997) *Understanding Attention Deficit Disorder: A Parent's Guide to ADD in Children*, 2nd edn. London: Random House.

Holowenko, H. (1999) *Attention Deficit/Hyperactivity Disorder: A Multi-disciplinary Approach*. London: Jessica Kingsley.

Hughes, L. and Cooper, P. (2007) *Understanding and Supporting Children with ADHD*. London: Paul Chapman Publishing.

Kendall, P. C. (2000) *Childhood Disorders*. East Sussex: Psychology Press.

Kewley, G. D. (1999) *Attention Deficit Hyperactivity Disorder: Recognition, Reality and Resolution*. London: David Fulton.

Kewley, G. D. (2005) *Attention Deficit Hyperactivity Disorder: What Can Teachers Do?*, 2nd edn. London: David Fulton.

Kirby, A., Davies, R. and Bryant, A. (2005) 'Do teachers know more about specific learning difficulties than general practitioners?', *British Journal of Special Education*, 32 (3): 122–6.

Lawrence, D. (1996) *Enhancing Self-esteem in the Classroom*, 2nd edn. London: Paul Chapman Publishing.

Lovey, J. (1999) 'ADHD in the classroom: a teacher's account', in P. Cooper and K. Bilton (eds), *Attention Deficit Hyperactivity Disorder (ADHD): Research, Practice and Opinion*. London: Whurr Publishers, pp. 170–84.

Medcalf, R., Marshall, J. and Rhoden, C. (2006) 'Exploring the relationship between physical education and enhancing behaviour in pupils with emotional behavioural difficulties', *Support for Learning*, 21 (4): 169–74.

Moline, S. and Frankenberger, W. (2001) 'Use of stimulant medication for treatment of attention deficit hyperactivity disorder: a survey of middle and high school students' attitudes', *Psychology in the Schools*, 38 (6): 569–84.

Munden, A. and Arcelus, J. (1999) *The AD/HD Handbook: A Guide for Parents and Professionals on Attention Deficit/Hyperactivity Disorder*. London: Jessica Kingsley.

National Institute for Clinical Excellence (NICE) (2000) *Guidance on the Use of Methylphenidate (Ritalin, Equasym) for Attention Deficit/Hyperactivity Disorder (ADHD) in Childhood*. London: NICE.

National Institute for Clinical Excellence (NICE) (2006) *Methylphenidate, Atomoxetine and Dexamfetamine for Attention Deficit Hyperactivity Disorder (ADHD) in Children and Adolescents*. London: NICE.

National Institute for Health and Clinical Excellence (NICE) (2008) *Attention Deficit Hyperactivity Disorder: Diagnosis and Management of ADHD in Children, Young People and Adults*. London: NICE.

NHS Quality Improvement Scotland (2008) *Attention Deficit and Hyperkinetic Disorders Services over Scotland: Report of the Implementation Review Exercise*. Scotland: NHS.

O'Regan, F. (2002) *How to Teach and Manage Children with ADHD*. Cambridge: LDA.

O'Regan, F. (2005) *ADHD*. London: Continuum.

Ratey, J. (2004) *The Neurobiology of ADHD*. Paper presented at the Sixth International ADDISS Conference, Liverpool, March.

Robin, A. L. (1998) *ADHD in Adolescents: Diagnosis and Treatment*. New York: Guilford Press.

Scottish Intercollegiate Guidelines Network (SIGN) (2001) *Attention Deficit and Hyperkinetic Disorders in Children and Young People: A National Clinical Guideline*. Edinburgh: SIGN.

Shaw, R., Grayson, A. and Lewis, V. (2005) 'Inhibition, ADHD and computer games: the inhibitory performance of children with ADHD on computerized tasks and games', *Journal of Attention Disorders*, 8 (4): 160–8.

Spohrer, K. E. (2002) *Supporting Children with Attention Deficit Hyperactivity Disorder*. Birmingham: Questions Publishing.

Stewart, W. (2006) 'Can you handle overactive pupils?', *Times Educational Supplement*, 1 December, p. 23.

Steyn, B. J., Schneider, J. and McArdle, P. (2002) 'The role of Disability Living Allowance in the management of attention deficit/hyperactivity disorder', *Child: Care, Health and Development*, 28 (6): 523–7.

Taylor, E. and Hemsley, R. (1995) 'Treating hyperkinetic disorders in childhood', *British Medical Journal*, 310, 1617–18.

Timimi, S. and 33 co-endorsers (2004) 'A Critique of the International Consensus Statement on ADHD', *Clinical Child and Family Psychology Review*, 7 (1): 59–63.

Uniview (2003) *Attention Difficulties: Practical Strategies for the Primary Classroom* [Videotape]. Wirral: Uniview.

Wheeler, L. (1996) 'The Influence of Self-Esteem on the Learning Experiences of Children'. Unpublished MA thesis.

Wheeler, L. (2007) *Attention Deficit Hyperactivity Disorder (ADHD): Identification, Assessment, Contextual and Curricular Variability in Boys at KS1 and KS2 in Mainstream Schools*. PhD thesis, University of Worcester.

Wheeler, L., Pumfrey, P. and Wakefield, P. (2009) 'Variability of ADHD symptoms across primary school contexts: an in-depth case study', *Emotional and Behavioural Difficulties*, 14 (1): 69–84.

Wheeler, L., Pumfrey, P., Wakefield, P. and Quill, W. (2008) 'ADHD in schools: prevalence, multi-professional involvements and school training needs in an LEA', *Emotional and Behavioural Difficulties*, 13 (3): 163–77.

World Health Organisation (1990) *International Classification of Diseases*, 10th edn. Geneva: WHO.

Index

Exciting Early Years and Primary Texts from SAGE

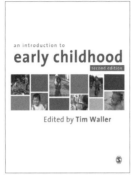

978-1-84787-518-1

978-1-84787-393-4

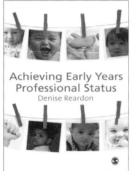

978-1-84787-190-9

978-1-84787-524-2

978-1-84860-127-7

978-1-84787-593-8

978-1-84860-119-2

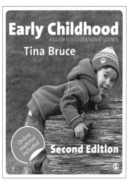

978-1-84860-224-3

978-1-84860-197-0

Find out more about these titles and our wide range of books for education students and practitioners at **www.sagepub.co.uk/education**

Exciting Education Texts from SAGE

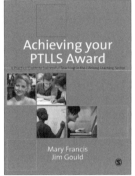

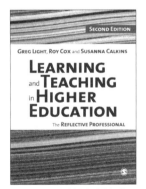

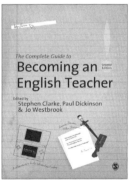